C-1754 CAREER EXAMINATION SERIES

This is your
PASSBOOK for...

Administrative Manager

Test Preparation Study Guide
Questions & Answers

NLC®

NATIONAL LEARNING CORPORATION®

National Learning Corporation

212 Michael Drive, Syosset, NY 11791
(516) 921-8888 • www.passbooks.com
E-mail: info@passbooks.com

PUBLISHED IN THE UNITED STATES OF AMERICA

PASSBOOK® SERIES

THE *PASSBOOK® SERIES* has been created to prepare applicants and candidates for the ultimate academic battlefield – the examination room.

At some time in our lives, each and every one of us may be required to take an examination – for validation, matriculation, admission, qualification, registration, certification, or licensure.

Based on the assumption that every applicant or candidate has met the basic formal educational standards, has taken the required number of courses, and read the necessary texts, the *PASSBOOK® SERIES* furnishes the one special preparation which may assure passing with confidence, instead of failing with insecurity. Examination questions – together with answers – are furnished as the basic vehicle for study so that the mysteries of the examination and its compounding difficulties may be eliminated or diminished by a sure method.

This book is meant to help you pass your examination provided that you qualify and are serious in your objective.

The entire field is reviewed through the huge store of content information which is succinctly presented through a provocative and challenging approach – the question-and-answer method.

A climate of success is established by furnishing the correct answers at the end of each test.

You soon learn to recognize types of questions, forms of questions, and patterns of questioning. You may even begin to anticipate expected outcomes.

You perceive that many questions are repeated or adapted so that you can gain acute insights, which may enable you to score many sure points.

You learn how to confront new questions, or types of questions, and to attack them confidently and work out the correct answers.

You note objectives and emphases, and recognize pitfalls and dangers, so that you may make positive educational adjustments.

Moreover, you are kept fully informed in relation to new concepts, methods, practices, and directions in the field.

You discover that you are actually taking the examination all the time: you are preparing for the examination by "taking" an examination, not by reading extraneous and/or supererogatory textbooks.

In short, this PASSBOOK®, used directedly, should be an important factor in helping you to pass your test.

ADMINISTRATIVE MANAGER

DUTIES AND RESPONSIBILITIES

Under direction, with great latitude for the exercise of independent judgment, is responsible for all the major areas of administration of a small agency; or several major areas of administration, such as personnel and budget, of one of the smaller departments; or one function in a major area of administration in an extraordinarily large department; or one major area of administration, such as personnel, in a large department; or assignments equivalent to those described; performs related work.

Under general direction, with great latitude for the exercise of independent judgment, serves as the principal assistant to the head of business administration of an extraordinarily large department; or as the principal assistant to the head of administration of a large department; or is responsible for preparing the expense budget of an extraordinarily large agency; or assignments equivalent to those described; performs related work.

Under general direction, with very great latitude for the exercise of independent judgment, serves as head of business administration of an extraordinarily large department; or as head of administration of a large department; or as executive officer of a medium size agency; or as head of administration of an agency engaged in missions of wide scope; or assignments equivalent to those described; performs related work.

Under general direction, with very great latitude for the exercise of independent judgment, serves as director of personnel administration of an extraordinarily large agency; or assignments equivalent to that described; performs related work.

TESTS

The written test will be of the multiple-choice type and may include questions on administration, supervision and management functions; personnel techniques and rules; training methods and techniques; budget preparation and administration, government operations and relationships; reading comprehension and interpretation of pertinent material; technical vocabulary; communications; human relations; and other related areas.

HOW TO TAKE A TEST

I. YOU MUST PASS AN EXAMINATION

A. WHAT EVERY CANDIDATE SHOULD KNOW

Examination applicants often ask us for help in preparing for the written test. What can I study in advance? What kinds of questions will be asked? How will the test be given? How will the papers be graded?

As an applicant for a civil service examination, you may be wondering about some of these things. Our purpose here is to suggest effective methods of advance study and to describe civil service examinations.

Your chances for success on this examination can be increased if you know how to prepare. Those "pre-examination jitters" can be reduced if you know what to expect. You can even experience an adventure in good citizenship if you know why civil service exams are given.

B. WHY ARE CIVIL SERVICE EXAMINATIONS GIVEN?

Civil service examinations are important to you in two ways. As a citizen, you want public jobs filled by employees who know how to do their work. As a job seeker, you want a fair chance to compete for that job on an equal footing with other candidates. The best-known means of accomplishing this two-fold goal is the competitive examination.

Exams are widely publicized throughout the nation. They may be administered for jobs in federal, state, city, municipal, town or village governments or agencies.

Any citizen may apply, with some limitations, such as the age or residence of applicants. Your experience and education may be reviewed to see whether you meet the requirements for the particular examination. When these requirements exist, they are reasonable and applied consistently to all applicants. Thus, a competitive examination may cause you some uneasiness now, but it is your privilege and safeguard.

C. HOW ARE CIVIL SERVICE EXAMS DEVELOPED?

Examinations are carefully written by trained technicians who are specialists in the field known as "psychological measurement," in consultation with recognized authorities in the field of work that the test will cover. These experts recommend the subject matter areas or skills to be tested; only those knowledges or skills important to your success on the job are included. The most reliable books and source materials available are used as references. Together, the experts and technicians judge the difficulty level of the questions.

Test technicians know how to phrase questions so that the problem is clearly stated. Their ethics do not permit "trick" or "catch" questions. Questions may have been tried out on sample groups, or subjected to statistical analysis, to determine their usefulness.

Written tests are often used in combination with performance tests, ratings of training and experience, and oral interviews. All of these measures combine to form the best-known means of finding the right person for the right job.

II. HOW TO PASS THE WRITTEN TEST

A. NATURE OF THE EXAMINATION

To prepare intelligently for civil service examinations, you should know how they differ from school examinations you have taken. In school you were assigned certain definite pages to read or subjects to cover. The examination questions were quite detailed and usually emphasized memory. Civil service exams, on the other hand, try to discover your present ability to perform the duties of a position, plus your potentiality to learn these duties. In other words, a civil service exam attempts to predict how successful you will be. Questions cover such a broad area that they cannot be as minute and detailed as school exam questions.

In the public service similar kinds of work, or positions, are grouped together in one "class." This process is known as *position-classification.* All the positions in a class are paid according to the salary range for that class. One class title covers all of these positions, and they are all tested by the same examination.

B. FOUR BASIC STEPS

1) Study the announcement

How, then, can you know what subjects to study? Our best answer is: "Learn as much as possible about the class of positions for which you've applied." The exam will test the knowledge, skills and abilities needed to do the work.

Your most valuable source of information about the position you want is the official exam announcement. This announcement lists the training and experience qualifications. Check these standards and apply only if you come reasonably close to meeting them.

The brief description of the position in the examination announcement offers some clues to the subjects which will be tested. Think about the job itself. Review the duties in your mind. Can you perform them, or are there some in which you are rusty? Fill in the blank spots in your preparation.

Many jurisdictions preview the written test in the exam announcement by including a section called "Knowledge and Abilities Required," "Scope of the Examination," or some similar heading. Here you will find out specifically what fields will be tested.

2) Review your own background

Once you learn in general what the position is all about, and what you need to know to do the work, ask yourself which subjects you already know fairly well and which need improvement. You may wonder whether to concentrate on improving your strong areas or on building some background in your fields of weakness. When the announcement has specified "some knowledge" or "considerable knowledge," or has used adjectives like "beginning principles of..." or "advanced ... methods," you can get a clue as to the number and difficulty of questions to be asked in any given field. More questions, and hence broader coverage, would be included for those subjects which are more important in the work. Now weigh your strengths and weaknesses against the job requirements and prepare accordingly.

3) Determine the level of the position

Another way to tell how intensively you should prepare is to understand the level of the job for which you are applying. Is it the entering level? In other words, is this the position in which beginners in a field of work are hired? Or is it an intermediate or advanced level? Sometimes this is indicated by such words as "Junior" or "Senior" in the class title. Other jurisdictions use Roman numerals to designate the level – Clerk I, Clerk II, for example. The word "Supervisor" sometimes appears in the title. If the level is not indicated by the title, check the description of duties. Will you be working under very close supervision, or will you have responsibility for independent decisions in this work?

4) Choose appropriate study materials

Now that you know the subjects to be examined and the relative amount of each subject to be covered, you can choose suitable study materials. For beginning level jobs, or even advanced ones, if you have a pronounced weakness in some aspect of your training, read a modern, standard textbook in that field. Be sure it is up to date and has general coverage. Such books are normally available at your library, and the librarian will be glad to help you locate one. For entry-level positions, questions of appropriate difficulty are chosen – neither highly advanced questions, nor those too simple. Such questions require careful thought but not advanced training.

If the position for which you are applying is technical or advanced, you will read more advanced, specialized material. If you are already familiar with the basic principles of your field, elementary textbooks would waste your time. Concentrate on advanced textbooks and technical periodicals. Think through the concepts and review difficult problems in your field.

These are all general sources. You can get more ideas on your own initiative, following these leads. For example, training manuals and publications of the government agency which employs workers in your field can be useful, particularly for technical and professional positions. A letter or visit to the government department involved may result in more specific study suggestions, and certainly will provide you with a more definite idea of the exact nature of the position you are seeking.

III. KINDS OF TESTS

Tests are used for purposes other than measuring knowledge and ability to perform specified duties. For some positions, it is equally important to test ability to make adjustments to new situations or to profit from training. In others, basic mental abilities not dependent on information are essential. Questions which test these things may not appear as pertinent to the duties of the position as those which test for knowledge and information. Yet they are often highly important parts of a fair examination. For very general questions, it is almost impossible to help you direct your study efforts. What we can do is to point out some of the more common of these general abilities needed in public service positions and describe some typical questions.

1) General information

Broad, general information has been found useful for predicting job success in some kinds of work. This is tested in a variety of ways, from vocabulary lists to questions about current events. Basic background in some field of work, such as sociology or economics, may be sampled in a group of questions. Often these are principles which have become familiar to most persons through exposure rather than through formal training. It is difficult to advise you how to study for these questions; being alert to the world around you is our best suggestion.

2) Verbal ability

An example of an ability needed in many positions is verbal or language ability. Verbal ability is, in brief, the ability to use and understand words. Vocabulary and grammar tests are typical measures of this ability. Reading comprehension or paragraph interpretation questions are common in many kinds of civil service tests. You are given a paragraph of written material and asked to find its central meaning.

3) Numerical ability

Number skills can be tested by the familiar arithmetic problem, by checking paired lists of numbers to see which are alike and which are different, or by interpreting charts and graphs. In the latter test, a graph may be printed in the test booklet which you are asked to use as the basis for answering questions.

4) Observation

A popular test for law-enforcement positions is the observation test. A picture is shown to you for several minutes, then taken away. Questions about the picture test your ability to observe both details and larger elements.

5) Following directions

In many positions in the public service, the employee must be able to carry out written instructions dependably and accurately. You may be given a chart with several columns, each column listing a variety of information. The questions require you to carry out directions involving the information given in the chart.

6) Skills and aptitudes

Performance tests effectively measure some manual skills and aptitudes. When the skill is one in which you are trained, such as typing or shorthand, you can practice. These tests are often very much like those given in business school or high school courses. For many of the other skills and aptitudes, however, no short-time preparation can be made. Skills and abilities natural to you or that you have developed throughout your lifetime are being tested.

Many of the general questions just described provide all the data needed to answer the questions and ask you to use your reasoning ability to find the answers. Your best preparation for these tests, as well as for tests of facts and ideas, is to be at your physical and mental best. You, no doubt, have your own methods of getting into an exam-taking mood and keeping "in shape." The next section lists some ideas on this subject.

IV. KINDS OF QUESTIONS

Only rarely is the "essay" question, which you answer in narrative form, used in civil service tests. Civil service tests are usually of the short-answer type. Full instructions for answering these questions will be given to you at the examination. But in case this is your first experience with short-answer questions and separate answer sheets, here is what you need to know:

1) Multiple-choice Questions

Most popular of the short-answer questions is the "multiple choice" or "best answer" question. It can be used, for example, to test for factual knowledge, ability to solve problems or judgment in meeting situations found at work.

A multiple-choice question is normally one of three types—

- It can begin with an incomplete statement followed by several possible endings. You are to find the one ending which *best* completes the statement, although some of the others may not be entirely wrong.
- It can also be a complete statement in the form of a question which is answered by choosing one of the statements listed.

- It can be in the form of a problem – again you select the best answer.

Here is an example of a multiple-choice question with a discussion which should give you some clues as to the method for choosing the right answer:

When an employee has a complaint about his assignment, the action which will *best* help him overcome his difficulty is to

A. discuss his difficulty with his coworkers
B. take the problem to the head of the organization
C. take the problem to the person who gave him the assignment
D. say nothing to anyone about his complaint

In answering this question, you should study each of the choices to find which is best. Consider choice "A" – Certainly an employee may discuss his complaint with fellow employees, but no change or improvement can result, and the complaint remains unresolved. Choice "B" is a poor choice since the head of the organization probably does not know what assignment you have been given, and taking your problem to him is known as "going over the head" of the supervisor. The supervisor, or person who made the assignment, is the person who can clarify it or correct any injustice. Choice "C" is, therefore, correct. To say nothing, as in choice "D," is unwise. Supervisors have and interest in knowing the problems employees are facing, and the employee is seeking a solution to his problem.

2) True/False Questions

The "true/false" or "right/wrong" form of question is sometimes used. Here a complete statement is given. Your job is to decide whether the statement is right or wrong.

SAMPLE: A roaming cell-phone call to a nearby city costs less than a non-roaming call to a distant city.

This statement is wrong, or false, since roaming calls are more expensive.

This is not a complete list of all possible question forms, although most of the others are variations of these common types. You will always get complete directions for answering questions. Be sure you understand *how* to mark your answers – ask questions until you do.

V. RECORDING YOUR ANSWERS

Computer terminals are used more and more today for many different kinds of exams.

For an examination with very few applicants, you may be told to record your answers in the test booklet itself. Separate answer sheets are much more common. If this separate answer sheet is to be scored by machine – and this is often the case – it is highly important that you mark your answers correctly in order to get credit.

An electronic scoring machine is often used in civil service offices because of the speed with which papers can be scored. Machine-scored answer sheets must be marked with a pencil, which will be given to you. This pencil has a high graphite content which responds to the electronic scoring machine. As a matter of fact, stray dots may register as answers, so do not let your pencil rest on the answer sheet while you are pondering the correct answer. Also, if your pencil lead breaks or is otherwise defective, ask for another.

Since the answer sheet will be dropped in a slot in the scoring machine, be careful not to bend the corners or get the paper crumpled.

The answer sheet normally has five vertical columns of numbers, with 30 numbers to a column. These numbers correspond to the question numbers in your test booklet. After each number, going across the page are four or five pairs of dotted lines. These short dotted lines have small letters or numbers above them. The first two pairs may also have a "T" or "F" above the letters. This indicates that the first two pairs only are to be used if the questions are of the true-false type. If the questions are multiple choice, disregard the "T" and "F" and pay attention only to the small letters or numbers.

Answer your questions in the manner of the sample that follows:

32. The largest city in the United States is
    A. Washington, D.C.
    B. New York City
    C. Chicago
    D. Detroit
    E. San Francisco

1) Choose the answer you think is best. (New York City is the largest, so "B" is correct.)
2) Find the row of dotted lines numbered the same as the question you are answering. (Find row number 32)
3) Find the pair of dotted lines corresponding to the answer. (Find the pair of lines under the mark "B.")
4) Make a solid black mark between the dotted lines.

VI. BEFORE THE TEST

Common sense will help you find procedures to follow to get ready for an examination. Too many of us, however, overlook these sensible measures. Indeed, nervousness and fatigue have been found to be the most serious reasons why applicants fail to do their best on civil service tests. Here is a list of reminders:

- Begin your preparation early – Don't wait until the last minute to go scurrying around for books and materials or to find out what the position is all about.
- Prepare continuously – An hour a night for a week is better than an all-night cram session. This has been definitely established. What is more, a night a week for a month will return better dividends than crowding your study into a shorter period of time.
- Locate the place of the exam – You have been sent a notice telling you when and where to report for the examination. If the location is in a different town or otherwise unfamiliar to you, it would be well to inquire the best route and learn something about the building.
- Relax the night before the test – Allow your mind to rest. Do not study at all that night. Plan some mild recreation or diversion; then go to bed early and get a good night's sleep.
- Get up early enough to make a leisurely trip to the place for the test – This way unforeseen events, traffic snarls, unfamiliar buildings, etc. will not upset you.
- Dress comfortably – A written test is not a fashion show. You will be known by number and not by name, so wear something comfortable.

- Leave excess paraphernalia at home – Shopping bags and odd bundles will get in your way. You need bring only the items mentioned in the official notice you received; usually everything you need is provided. Do not bring reference books to the exam. They will only confuse those last minutes and be taken away from you when in the test room.
- Arrive somewhat ahead of time – If because of transportation schedules you must get there very early, bring a newspaper or magazine to take your mind off yourself while waiting.
- Locate the examination room – When you have found the proper room, you will be directed to the seat or part of the room where you will sit. Sometimes you are given a sheet of instructions to read while you are waiting. Do not fill out any forms until you are told to do so; just read them and be prepared.
- Relax and prepare to listen to the instructions
- If you have any physical problem that may keep you from doing your best, be sure to tell the test administrator. If you are sick or in poor health, you really cannot do your best on the exam. You can come back and take the test some other time.

VII. AT THE TEST

The day of the test is here and you have the test booklet in your hand. The temptation to get going is very strong. Caution! There is more to success than knowing the right answers. You must know how to identify your papers and understand variations in the type of short-answer question used in this particular examination. Follow these suggestions for maximum results from your efforts:

1) Cooperate with the monitor

The test administrator has a duty to create a situation in which you can be as much at ease as possible. He will give instructions, tell you when to begin, check to see that you are marking your answer sheet correctly, and so on. He is not there to guard you, although he will see that your competitors do not take unfair advantage. He wants to help you do your best.

2) Listen to all instructions

Don't jump the gun! Wait until you understand all directions. In most civil service tests you get more time than you need to answer the questions. So don't be in a hurry. Read each word of instructions until you clearly understand the meaning. Study the examples, listen to all announcements and follow directions. Ask questions if you do not understand what to do.

3) Identify your papers

Civil service exams are usually identified by number only. You will be assigned a number; you must not put your name on your test papers. Be sure to copy your number correctly. Since more than one exam may be given, copy your exact examination title.

4) Plan your time

Unless you are told that a test is a "speed" or "rate of work" test, speed itself is usually not important. Time enough to answer all the questions will be provided, but this does not mean that you have all day. An overall time limit has been set. Divide the total time (in minutes) by the number of questions to determine the approximate time you have for each question.

5) Do not linger over difficult questions

If you come across a difficult question, mark it with a paper clip (useful to have along) and come back to it when you have been through the booklet. One caution if you do this – be sure to skip a number on your answer sheet as well. Check often to be sure that you have not lost your place and that you are marking in the row numbered the same as the question you are answering.

6) Read the questions

Be sure you know what the question asks! Many capable people are unsuccessful because they failed to *read* the questions correctly.

7) Answer all questions

Unless you have been instructed that a penalty will be deducted for incorrect answers, it is better to guess than to omit a question.

8) Speed tests

It is often better NOT to guess on speed tests. It has been found that on timed tests people are tempted to spend the last few seconds before time is called in marking answers at random – without even reading them – in the hope of picking up a few extra points. To discourage this practice, the instructions may warn you that your score will be "corrected" for guessing. That is, a penalty will be applied. The incorrect answers will be deducted from the correct ones, or some other penalty formula will be used.

9) Review your answers

If you finish before time is called, go back to the questions you guessed or omitted to give them further thought. Review other answers if you have time.

10) Return your test materials

If you are ready to leave before others have finished or time is called, take ALL your materials to the monitor and leave quietly. Never take any test material with you. The monitor can discover whose papers are not complete, and taking a test booklet may be grounds for disqualification.

VIII. EXAMINATION TECHNIQUES

1) Read the general instructions carefully. These are usually printed on the first page of the exam booklet. As a rule, these instructions refer to the timing of the examination; the fact that you should not start work until the signal and must stop work at a signal, etc. If there are any *special* instructions, such as a choice of questions to be answered, make sure that you note this instruction carefully.

2) When you are ready to start work on the examination, that is as soon as the signal has been given, read the instructions to each question booklet, underline any key words or phrases, such as *least, best, outline, describe* and the like. In this way you will tend to answer as requested rather than discover on reviewing your paper that you *listed without describing*, that you selected the *worst* choice rather than the *best* choice, etc.

3) If the examination is of the objective or multiple-choice type – that is, each question will also give a series of possible answers: A, B, C or D, and you are called upon to select the best answer and write the letter next to that answer on your answer paper – it is advisable to start answering each question in turn. There may be anywhere from 50 to 100 such questions in the three or four hours allotted and you can see how much time would be taken if you read through all the questions before beginning to answer any. Furthermore, if you come across a question or group of questions which you know would be difficult to answer, it would undoubtedly affect your handling of all the other questions.

4) If the examination is of the essay type and contains but a few questions, it is a moot point as to whether you should read all the questions before starting to answer any one. Of course, if you are given a choice – say five out of seven and the like – then it is essential to read all the questions so you can eliminate the two that are most difficult. If, however, you are asked to answer all the questions, there may be danger in trying to answer the easiest one first because you may find that you will spend too much time on it. The best technique is to answer the first question, then proceed to the second, etc.

5) Time your answers. Before the exam begins, write down the time it started, then add the time allowed for the examination and write down the time it must be completed, then divide the time available somewhat as follows:
   - If 3-1/2 hours are allowed, that would be 210 minutes. If you have 80 objective-type questions, that would be an average of 2-1/2 minutes per question. Allow yourself no more than 2 minutes per question, or a total of 160 minutes, which will permit about 50 minutes to review.
   - If for the time allotment of 210 minutes there are 7 essay questions to answer, that would average about 30 minutes a question. Give yourself only 25 minutes per question so that you have about 35 minutes to review.

6) The most important instruction is to *read each question* and make sure you know what is wanted. The second most important instruction is to *time yourself properly* so that you answer every question. The third most important instruction is to *answer every question*. Guess if you have to but include something for each question. Remember that you will receive no credit for a blank and will probably receive some credit if you write something in answer to an essay question. If you guess a letter – say "B" for a multiple-choice question – you may have guessed right. If you leave a blank as an answer to a multiple-choice question, the examiners may respect your feelings but it will not add a point to your score. Some exams may penalize you for wrong answers, so in such cases *only*, you may not want to guess unless you have some basis for your answer.

7) Suggestions
   a. Objective-type questions
      1. Examine the question booklet for proper sequence of pages and questions
      2. Read all instructions carefully
      3. Skip any question which seems too difficult; return to it after all other questions have been answered
      4. Apportion your time properly; do not spend too much time on any single question or group of questions

5. Note and underline key words – *all, most, fewest, least, best, worst, same, opposite,* etc.
6. Pay particular attention to negatives
7. Note unusual option, e.g., unduly long, short, complex, different or similar in content to the body of the question
8. Observe the use of "hedging" words – *probably, may, most likely,* etc.
9. Make sure that your answer is put next to the same number as the question
10. Do not second-guess unless you have good reason to believe the second answer is definitely more correct
11. Cross out original answer if you decide another answer is more accurate; do not erase until you are ready to hand your paper in
12. Answer all questions; guess unless instructed otherwise
13. Leave time for review

b. Essay questions
   1. Read each question carefully
   2. Determine exactly what is wanted. Underline key words or phrases.
   3. Decide on outline or paragraph answer
   4. Include many different points and elements unless asked to develop any one or two points or elements
   5. Show impartiality by giving pros and cons unless directed to select one side only
   6. Make and write down any assumptions you find necessary to answer the questions
   7. Watch your English, grammar, punctuation and choice of words
   8. Time your answers; don't crowd material

8) Answering the essay question

Most essay questions can be answered by framing the specific response around several key words or ideas. Here are a few such key words or ideas:

M's: manpower, materials, methods, money, management
P's: purpose, program, policy, plan, procedure, practice, problems, pitfalls, personnel, public relations

a. Six basic steps in handling problems:
   1. Preliminary plan and background development
   2. Collect information, data and facts
   3. Analyze and interpret information, data and facts
   4. Analyze and develop solutions as well as make recommendations
   5. Prepare report and sell recommendations
   6. Install recommendations and follow up effectiveness

b. Pitfalls to avoid
   1. *Taking things for granted* – A statement of the situation does not necessarily imply that each of the elements is necessarily true; for example, a complaint may be invalid and biased so that all that can be taken for granted is that a complaint has been registered

2. *Considering only one side of a situation* – Wherever possible, indicate several alternatives and then point out the reasons you selected the best one
3. *Failing to indicate follow up* – Whenever your answer indicates action on your part, make certain that you will take proper follow-up action to see how successful your recommendations, procedures or actions turn out to be
4. *Taking too long in answering any single question* – Remember to time your answers properly

IX. AFTER THE TEST

Scoring procedures differ in detail among civil service jurisdictions although the general principles are the same. Whether the papers are hand-scored or graded by machine we have described, they are nearly always graded by number. That is, the person who marks the paper knows only the number – never the name – of the applicant. Not until all the papers have been graded will they be matched with names. If other tests, such as training and experience or oral interview ratings have been given, scores will be combined. Different parts of the examination usually have different weights. For example, the written test might count 60 percent of the final grade, and a rating of training and experience 40 percent. In many jurisdictions, veterans will have a certain number of points added to their grades.

After the final grade has been determined, the names are placed in grade order and an eligible list is established. There are various methods for resolving ties between those who get the same final grade – probably the most common is to place first the name of the person whose application was received first. Job offers are made from the eligible list in the order the names appear on it. You will be notified of your grade and your rank as soon as all these computations have been made. This will be done as rapidly as possible.

People who are found to meet the requirements in the announcement are called "eligibles." Their names are put on a list of eligible candidates. An eligible's chances of getting a job depend on how high he stands on this list and how fast agencies are filling jobs from the list.

When a job is to be filled from a list of eligibles, the agency asks for the names of people on the list of eligibles for that job. When the civil service commission receives this request, it sends to the agency the names of the three people highest on this list. Or, if the job to be filled has specialized requirements, the office sends the agency the names of the top three persons who meet these requirements from the general list.

The appointing officer makes a choice from among the three people whose names were sent to him. If the selected person accepts the appointment, the names of the others are put back on the list to be considered for future openings.

That is the rule in hiring from all kinds of eligible lists, whether they are for typist, carpenter, chemist, or something else. For every vacancy, the appointing officer has his choice of any one of the top three eligibles on the list. This explains why the person whose name is on top of the list sometimes does not get an appointment when some of the persons lower on the list do. If the appointing officer chooses the second or third eligible, the No. 1 eligible does not get a job at once, but stays on the list until he is appointed or the list is terminated.

X. HOW TO PASS THE INTERVIEW TEST

The examination for which you applied requires an oral interview test. You have already taken the written test and you are now being called for the interview test – the final part of the formal examination.

You may think that it is not possible to prepare for an interview test and that there are no procedures to follow during an interview. Our purpose is to point out some things you can do in advance that will help you and some good rules to follow and pitfalls to avoid while you are being interviewed.

What is an interview supposed to test?

The written examination is designed to test the technical knowledge and competence of the candidate; the oral is designed to evaluate intangible qualities, not readily measured otherwise, and to establish a list showing the relative fitness of each candidate – as measured against his competitors – for the position sought. Scoring is not on the basis of "right" and "wrong," but on a sliding scale of values ranging from "not passable" to "outstanding." As a matter of fact, it is possible to achieve a relatively low score without a single "incorrect" answer because of evident weakness in the qualities being measured.

Occasionally, an examination may consist entirely of an oral test – either an individual or a group oral. In such cases, information is sought concerning the technical knowledges and abilities of the candidate, since there has been no written examination for this purpose. More commonly, however, an oral test is used to supplement a written examination.

Who conducts interviews?

The composition of oral boards varies among different jurisdictions. In nearly all, a representative of the personnel department serves as chairman. One of the members of the board may be a representative of the department in which the candidate would work. In some cases, "outside experts" are used, and, frequently, a businessman or some other representative of the general public is asked to serve. Labor and management or other special groups may be represented. The aim is to secure the services of experts in the appropriate field.

However the board is composed, it is a good idea (and not at all improper or unethical) to ascertain in advance of the interview who the members are and what groups they represent. When you are introduced to them, you will have some idea of their backgrounds and interests, and at least you will not stutter and stammer over their names.

What should be done before the interview?

While knowledge about the board members is useful and takes some of the surprise element out of the interview, there is other preparation which is more substantive. It *is* possible to prepare for an oral interview – in several ways:

1) Keep a copy of your application and review it carefully before the interview

This may be the only document before the oral board, and the starting point of the interview. Know what education and experience you have listed there, and the sequence and dates of all of it. Sometimes the board will ask you to review the highlights of your experience for them; you should not have to hem and haw doing it.

2) Study the class specification and the examination announcement

Usually, the oral board has one or both of these to guide them. The qualities, characteristics or knowledges required by the position sought are stated in these documents. They offer valuable clues as to the nature of the oral interview. For example, if the job involves supervisory responsibilities, the announcement will usually indicate that knowledge of modern supervisory methods and the qualifications of the candidate as a supervisor will be tested. If so, you can expect such questions, frequently in the form of a hypothetical situation which you are expected to solve. NEVER go into an oral without knowledge of the duties and responsibilities of the job you seek.

3) Think through each qualification required

Try to visualize the kind of questions you would ask if you were a board member. How well could you answer them? Try especially to appraise your own knowledge and background in each area, *measured against the job sought*, and identify any areas in which you are weak. Be critical and realistic – do not flatter yourself.

4) Do some general reading in areas in which you feel you may be weak

For example, if the job involves supervision and your past experience has NOT, some general reading in supervisory methods and practices, particularly in the field of human relations, might be useful. Do NOT study agency procedures or detailed manuals. The oral board will be testing your understanding and capacity, not your memory.

5) Get a good night's sleep and watch your general health and mental attitude

You will want a clear head at the interview. Take care of a cold or any other minor ailment, and of course, no hangovers.

What should be done on the day of the interview?

Now comes the day of the interview itself. Give yourself plenty of time to get there. Plan to arrive somewhat ahead of the scheduled time, particularly if your appointment is in the fore part of the day. If a previous candidate fails to appear, the board might be ready for you a bit early. By early afternoon an oral board is almost invariably behind schedule if there are many candidates, and you may have to wait. Take along a book or magazine to read, or your application to review, but leave any extraneous material in the waiting room when you go in for your interview. In any event, relax and compose yourself.

The matter of dress is important. The board is forming impressions about you – from your experience, your manners, your attitude, and your appearance. Give your personal appearance careful attention. Dress your best, but not your flashiest. Choose conservative, appropriate clothing, and be sure it is immaculate. This is a business interview, and your appearance should indicate that you regard it as such. Besides, being well groomed and properly dressed will help boost your confidence.

Sooner or later, someone will call your name and escort you into the interview room. *This is it.* From here on you are on your own. It is too late for any more preparation. But remember, you asked for this opportunity to prove your fitness, and you are here because your request was granted.

What happens when you go in?

The usual sequence of events will be as follows: The clerk (who is often the board stenographer) will introduce you to the chairman of the oral board, who will introduce you to the other members of the board. Acknowledge the introductions before you sit down. Do not be surprised if you find a microphone facing you or a stenotypist sitting by. Oral interviews are usually recorded in the event of an appeal or other review.

Usually the chairman of the board will open the interview by reviewing the highlights of your education and work experience from your application – primarily for the benefit of the other members of the board, as well as to get the material into the record. Do not interrupt or comment unless there is an error or significant misinterpretation; if that is the case, do not hesitate. But do not quibble about insignificant matters. Also, he will usually ask you some question about your education, experience or your present job – partly to get you to start talking and to establish the interviewing "rapport." He may start the actual questioning, or turn it over to one of the other members. Frequently, each member undertakes the questioning on a particular area, one in which he is perhaps most competent, so you can expect each member to participate in the examination. Because time is limited, you may also expect some rather abrupt switches in the direction the questioning takes, so do not be upset by it. Normally, a board member will not pursue a single line of questioning unless he discovers a particular strength or weakness.

After each member has participated, the chairman will usually ask whether any member has any further questions, then will ask you if you have anything you wish to add. Unless you are expecting this question, it may floor you. Worse, it may start you off on an extended, extemporaneous speech. The board is not usually seeking more information. The question is principally to offer you a last opportunity to present further qualifications or to indicate that you have nothing to add. So, if you feel that a significant qualification or characteristic has been overlooked, it is proper to point it out in a sentence or so. Do not compliment the board on the thoroughness of their examination – they have been sketchy, and you know it. If you wish, merely say, "No thank you, I have nothing further to add." This is a point where you can "talk yourself out" of a good impression or fail to present an important bit of information. Remember, *you close the interview yourself.*

The chairman will then say, "That is all, Mr. _______, thank you." Do not be startled; the interview is over, and quicker than you think. Thank him, gather your belongings and take your leave. Save your sigh of relief for the other side of the door.

How to put your best foot forward

Throughout this entire process, you may feel that the board individually and collectively is trying to pierce your defenses, seek out your hidden weaknesses and embarrass and confuse you. Actually, this is not true. They are obliged to make an appraisal of your qualifications for the job you are seeking, and they want to see you in your best light. Remember, they must interview all candidates and a non-cooperative candidate may become a failure in spite of their best efforts to bring out his qualifications. Here are 15 suggestions that will help you:

1) Be natural – Keep your attitude confident, not cocky

If you are not confident that you can do the job, do not expect the board to be. Do not apologize for your weaknesses, try to bring out your strong points. The board is interested in a positive, not negative, presentation. Cockiness will antagonize any board member and make him wonder if you are covering up a weakness by a false show of strength.

2) Get comfortable, but don't lounge or sprawl

Sit erectly but not stiffly. A careless posture may lead the board to conclude that you are careless in other things, or at least that you are not impressed by the importance of the occasion. Either conclusion is natural, even if incorrect. Do not fuss with your clothing, a pencil or an ashtray. Your hands may occasionally be useful to emphasize a point; do not let them become a point of distraction.

3) Do not wisecrack or make small talk

This is a serious situation, and your attitude should show that you consider it as such. Further, the time of the board is limited – they do not want to waste it, and neither should you.

4) Do not exaggerate your experience or abilities

In the first place, from information in the application or other interviews and sources, the board may know more about you than you think. Secondly, you probably will not get away with it. An experienced board is rather adept at spotting such a situation, so do not take the chance.

5) If you know a board member, do not make a point of it, yet do not hide it

Certainly you are not fooling him, and probably not the other members of the board. Do not try to take advantage of your acquaintanceship – it will probably do you little good.

6) Do not dominate the interview

Let the board do that. They will give you the clues – do not assume that you have to do all the talking. Realize that the board has a number of questions to ask you, and do not try to take up all the interview time by showing off your extensive knowledge of the answer to the first one.

7) Be attentive

You only have 20 minutes or so, and you should keep your attention at its sharpest throughout. When a member is addressing a problem or question to you, give him your undivided attention. Address your reply principally to him, but do not exclude the other board members.

8) Do not interrupt

A board member may be stating a problem for you to analyze. He will ask you a question when the time comes. Let him state the problem, and wait for the question.

9) Make sure you understand the question

Do not try to answer until you are sure what the question is. If it is not clear, restate it in your own words or ask the board member to clarify it for you. However, do not haggle about minor elements.

10) Reply promptly but not hastily

A common entry on oral board rating sheets is "candidate responded readily," or "candidate hesitated in replies." Respond as promptly and quickly as you can, but do not jump to a hasty, ill-considered answer.

11) Do not be peremptory in your answers

A brief answer is proper – but do not fire your answer back. That is a losing game from your point of view. The board member can probably ask questions much faster than you can answer them.

12) Do not try to create the answer you think the board member wants

He is interested in what kind of mind you have and how it works – not in playing games. Furthermore, he can usually spot this practice and will actually grade you down on it.

13) Do not switch sides in your reply merely to agree with a board member

Frequently, a member will take a contrary position merely to draw you out and to see if you are willing and able to defend your point of view. Do not start a debate, yet do not surrender a good position. If a position is worth taking, it is worth defending.

14) Do not be afraid to admit an error in judgment if you are shown to be wrong

The board knows that you are forced to reply without any opportunity for careful consideration. Your answer may be demonstrably wrong. If so, admit it and get on with the interview.

15) Do not dwell at length on your present job

The opening question may relate to your present assignment. Answer the question but do not go into an extended discussion. You are being examined for a *new* job, not your present one. As a matter of fact, try to phrase ALL your answers in terms of the job for which you are being examined.

Basis of Rating

Probably you will forget most of these "do's" and "don'ts" when you walk into the oral interview room. Even remembering them all will not ensure you a passing grade. Perhaps you did not have the qualifications in the first place. But remembering them will help you to put your best foot forward, without treading on the toes of the board members.

Rumor and popular opinion to the contrary notwithstanding, an oral board wants you to make the best appearance possible. They know you are under pressure – but they also want to see how you respond to it as a guide to what your reaction would be under the pressures of the job you seek. They will be influenced by the degree of poise you display, the personal traits you show and the manner in which you respond.

ABOUT THIS BOOK

This book contains tests divided into Examination Sections. Go through each test, answering every question in the margin. We have also attached a sample answer sheet at the back of the book that can be removed and used. At the end of each test look at the answer key and check your answers. On the ones you got wrong, look at the right answer choice and learn. Do not fill in the answers first. Do not memorize the questions and answers, but understand the answer and principles involved. On your test, the questions will likely be different from the samples. Questions are changed and new ones added. If you understand these past questions you should have success with any changes that arise. Tests may consist of several types of questions. We have additional books on each subject should more study be advisable or necessary for you. Finally, the more you study, the better prepared you will be. This book is intended to be the last thing you study before you walk into the examination room. Prior study of relevant texts is also recommended. NLC publishes some of these in our Fundamental Series. Knowledge and good sense are important factors in passing your exam. Good luck also helps. So now study this Passbook, absorb the material contained within and take that knowledge into the examination. Then do your best to pass that exam.

EXAMINATION SECTION

EXAMINATION SECTION

TEST 1

DIRECTIONS: Each question or incomplete statement is followed by several suggested answers or completions. Select the one that BEST answers the question or completes the statement. *PRINT THE LETTER OF THE CORRECT ANSWER IN THE SPACE AT THE RIGHT.*

1. Assume that a manager is preparing a list of reasons to justify making a major change in methods and procedures in his agency. 1.____
Which of the following reasons would be LEAST appropriate on such a list?
   A. Improve the means for satisfying needs and wants of agency personnel
   B. Increase efficiency
   C. Intensify competition and stimulate loyalty to separate work groups
   D. Contribute to the individual and group satisfaction of agency personnel

2. Many managers recognize the benefits of decentralization but are concerned about the danger of over-relaxation of control as a result of increased delegation. 2.____
Of the following, the MOST appropriate means of establishing proper control under decentralization is for the manager to
   A. establish detailed standards for all phases of operation
   B. shift his attention from operating details to appraisal of results
   C. keep himself informed by decreasing the time span covered by reports
   D. make unilateral decisions on difficult situations that arise in decentralized locations

3. In some agencies, the counsel to the agency head is given the right to bypass the chain of command and issue orders directly to the staff concerning matters that involve certain specific processes and practices. 3.____
This situation MOST NEARLY illustrates the principle of _____ authority.
   A. the acceptance theory of
   B. multiple-linear
   C. splintered
   D. functional

4. Assume that a manager is writing a brief report to his superior outlining the advantages of matrix organization. 4.____
Of the following, it would be INCORRECT to state that
   A. in matrix organization, a project is emphasized by designating one individual as the focal point for all matters pertaining to it
   B. utilization of manpower can be flexible in matrix organization because a reservoir of specialists is maintained in the line operations
   C. the usual line staff arrangement is generally reversed in matrix organization
   D. in matrix organization, responsiveness to project needs is generally faster due to establishing needed communication lines and decision points

5. It is commonly understood that communication is an important part of the administrative process. 5.____
Which of the following is NOT a valid principle of the communication process in administration?
   A. The channels of communication should be spontaneous.
   B. The lines of communication should be as direct and as short as possible.
   C. Communications should be authenticated.
   D. The persons serving in communications centers should be competent.

6. The PRIMARY purpose of the quantitative approach in management is to 6.____
   A. identify better alternatives for management decision-making
   B. substitute data for judgment
   C. match opinions to data
   D. match data to opinions

7. If an executive wants to make a strong case for running his agency as a flat type of structure, he should point out that the PRIMARY advantage of doing so is to 7.____
   A. provide less experience in decision-making for agency personnel
   B. facilitate frequent contact between each superior and his immediate subordinates
   C. improve communication and unify attitudes
   D. improve communication and diversify attitudes

8. In deciding how detailed his delegation of authority to a subordinate should be, a manager should follow the general principle that 8.____
   A. delegation of authority is more detailed at the top of the organizational structure
   B. detailed delegation of authority is associated with detailed work assignments
   C. delegation of authority should be in sufficient detail to prevent overlapping assignments
   D. detailed delegation of authority is associated with broad work assignments

9. In recent years, newer and more fluid types of organizational forms have been developed. One of these is a type of free-form organization. 9.____
Another name for this type of organization is the
   A. project organization
   B. semimix organization
   C. naturalistic structure
   D. semipermanent structure

10. Which of the following is the MAJOR objective of operational or management systems audits? 10.____
   A. Determining the number of personnel needed
   B. Recommending opportunities for improving operating and management practices
   C. Detecting fraud
   D. Determining organization problems

11. Assume that a manager observes that conflict exists between his agency and another operating agency of government. 11.____
Which of the following statements is the LEAST probable cause of this conflict?
    A. Incompatibility between the agencies' goals but similarity in their resource allocations
    B. Compatibility between agencies' goals and resources
    C. Status differences between agency personnel
    D. Differences in perceptions of each other's policies

12. Of the following, a MAJOR purpose of brainstorming as a problem-solving technique is to 12.____
    A. develop the ability to concentrate
    B. encourage creative thinking
    C. evaluate employees' ideas
    D. develop critical ability

13. The one of the following requirements which is LEAST likely to accompany regular delegation of work from a manager to a subordinate is a(n) 13.____
    A. need to review the organization's workload
    B. indication of what work the subordinate is to do
    C. need to grant authority to the subordinate
    D. obligation for the subordinate who accepts the work to try to complete it

14. Of the following, the one factor which is generally considered LEAST essential to successful committee operation is 14.____
    A. stating a clear definition of the authority and scope of the committee
    B. selecting the committee chairman carefully
    C. limiting the size of the committee to four persons
    D. limiting the subject matter to that which can be handled in group discussion

15. In using the program evaluation and review technique, the *critical path* is the path that 15.____
    A. requires the shortest time
    B. requires the longest time
    C. focuses most attention on social constraints
    D. focuses most attention to repetitious jobs

16. Which one of the following is LEAST characteristic of the management-by-objectives approach? 16.____
    A. The scope within which the employee may exercise decision-making is broadened.
    B. The employee starts with a self-appraisal of his performances, abilities, and potential.
    C. Emphasis is placed on activities performed; activities orientation is maximized.
    D. Each employee participates in determining his own objectives.

17. The function of management which puts into effect the decisions, plans, and programs that have previously been worked out for achieving the goals of the group is MOST appropriately called 17.____
    A. scheduling B. classifying C. budgeting D. directing

18. In the establishment of a plan to improve office productive efficiency, which of the following guidelines is LEAST helpful in setting sound work standards? 18.____
    A. Employees must accept the plan's objectives.
    B. Current production averages must be promulgated as work standards for a group.
    C. The work flow must generally be fairly constant.
    D. The operation of the plan must be expressed in terms understandable to the worker.

19. The one of the following activities which, generally speaking, is of *relatively* MAJOR importance at the lower-management level and of *somewhat* LESSER importance at higher-management levels is 19.____
    A. actuating B. forecasting C. organizing D. planning

20. Three styles of leadership exist: democratic, authoritarian, and laissez-faire. Of the following work situations, the one in which a democratic approach would normally be the MOST effective is when the work is 20.____
    A. routine and moderately complex B. repetitious and simple
    C. complex and not routine D. simple and not routine

21. Governmental and business organizations *generally* encounter the GREATEST difficulties in developing tangible measures of which one of the following? 21.____
    A. The level of expenditures B. Contributions to social welfare
    C. Retention rates D. Causes of labor unrest

22. Of the following, a *management-by-objectives* program is BEST described as 22.____
    A. a new comprehensive plan of organization
    B. introduction of budgets and financial controls
    C. introduction of long-range planning
    D. development of future goals with supporting and related progress reviews

23. Research and analysis is probably the most widely used technique for selecting alternatives when major planning decisions are involved. 23.____
    Of the following, a VALUABLE characteristic of research and analysis is that this technique
    A. places the problem in a meaningful conceptual framework
    B. involves practical application of the various alternatives
    C. accurately analyzes all important tangibles
    D. is much less expensive than other problem-solving methods

24. If a manager were assigned the task of using a systems approach to designing a new work unit, which of the following should he consider FIRST in carrying out his design? 24.____
    A. Networks
    B. Work flows and information processes
    C. Linkages and relationships
    D. Decision points and control loops

25. The MAIN distinction between Theory X and Theory Y approaches to organization, in accordance with Douglas McGregor's view, is that Theory Y 25.____
    A. considers that work is natural to people; Theory X assumes that people are lazy and avoid work
    B. leads to a tall, narrow organization structure, while Theory X leads to one that is flat
    C. organizations motivate people with money; Theory X organizations motivate people with good working conditions
    D. represents authoritarian management, while Theory X management is participative

---

KEY (CORRECT ANSWERS)

1.	C	11.	B
2.	B	12.	B
3.	D	13.	A
4.	C	14.	C
5.	A	15.	B
6.	A	16.	C
7.	C	17.	D
8.	B	18.	B
9.	A	19.	A
10.	B	20.	C

21.	B
22.	D
23.	A
24.	B
25.	A

TEST 2

DIRECTIONS: Each question or incomplete statement is followed by several suggested answers or completions. Select the one that BEST answers the question or completes the statement. *PRINT THE LETTER OF THE CORRECT ANSWER IN THE SPACE AT THE RIGHT.*

1. Of the following, the stage in decision-making which is usually MOST difficult is 1.____
   A. stating the alternatives
   B. predicting the possible outcome of each alternative
   C. evaluating the relative merits of each alternative
   D. minimizing the undesirable aspects of the alternative selected

2. In a department where a clerk is reporting both to a senior clerk in charge of the mail room and also to a supervising clerk in charge of the duplicating section, there may be a breakdown of the management principle called 2.____
   A. horizontal specialization
   B. job enrichment
   C. unity of command
   D. Graicunas' Law

3. Of the following, the failure by line managers to accept and appreciate the benefits and limitations of a new program or system VERY frequently can be traced to the 3.____
   A. budgetary problems involved
   B. resultant need to reduce staff
   C. lack of controls it engenders
   D. failure of top management to support its implementation

4. Although there is general agreement that *management-by-objectives* has made a major contribution to modern management of large organizations, criticisms of the system during the past few years have resulted in 4.____
   A. mounting pressure for relaxation of management goals
   B. renewed concern with human values and the manager's personal needs
   C. over-mechanistic application of the perceptions of the behavioral scientists
   D. disillusionment with *management-by-objectives* on the part of a majority of managers

5. Of the following, which is usually considered to be a MAJOR obstacle to the systematic analysis of potential problems by managers? 5.____
   A. Managers have a tendency to think that all the implications of some proposed step cannot be fully understood.
   B. Rewards rarely go to those managers who are most successful at resolving current problems in management.
   C. There is a common conviction of manages that their goals are difficult to achieve.
   D. Managers are far more concerned about correcting today's problems than with preventing tomorrow's.

6. Which of the following should generally have the MOST influence on the selection of supervisors? 6.____
   A. Experience within the work unit where the vacancies exist
   B. Amount of money needed to effect the promotion
   C. Personal preferences of the administration
   D. Evaluation of capacity to exercise supervisory responsibilities

7. In questioning a potential administrator for selection purposes, the one of the following practices which is MOST desirable is to 7.____
   A. encourage the job applicant to give primarily *yes* or *no* replies
   B. get the applicant to talk freely and in detail about his background
   C. let the job applicant speak most of the time
   D. probe the applicant's attitudes, motivation, and willingness to accept responsibility

8. In implementing the managerial function of training subordinates, it is USEFUL to know that a widely agreed-upon definition of human learning is that learning 8.____
   A. is a relatively permanent change in behavior that results from reinforced practice or experience
   B. involves an improvement, but not necessarily a change in behavior
   C. involves a change in behavior, but not necessarily an improvement
   D. is a temporary change in behavior which must be subject to practice or experience

9. If a manager were thinking about using a committee of subordinates to solve an operating problem, which of the following would generally NOT be an advantage of such use of the committee approach? 9.____
   A. Improved coordination
   B. Low cost
   C. Increased motivation
   D. Integrated judgment

10. Which one of the following management approaches MOST often uses model-building techniques to solve management problems? 10.____
    ______ approach.
    A. Behavioral
    B. Fiscal
    C. Quantitative
    D. Process

11. Of the following, the MOST serious risk in using budgets as a tool for management control is the 11.____
    A. probable neglect of other good management practices
    B. likelihood of guesswork because of the need to plan far in advance
    C. possibility of undue emphasis on factors that are easiest to measure
    D. danger of making qualitative rather than quantitative assessments of performance

12. In government budgeting, the problem of relating financial transactions to the fiscal year in which they are budgeted is BEST met by 12.____
    A. determining the cash balance by comparing how much money has been received and how much has been paid out
    B. applying net revenue to the fiscal year in which they are collected as offset by relevant expenses

C. adopting a system whereby appropriations are entered when they are received and expenditures are entered when they are paid out
D. entering expenditures on the books when the obligation to make the expenditure is made

13. If the agency's bookkeeping system records income when it is received and expenditures when the money is paid out this system is USUALLY known as a _____ system. 13.____
A. cash
B. flow-payment
C. deferred
D. fiscal year income

14. An audit, as the term applies to budget execution, is MOST NEARLY a 14.____
A. procedure based on the budget estimates
B. control exercised by the executive on the legislature in the establishment of program priorities
C. check on the legality of expenditures and is based on the appropriations act
D. requirement which must be met before funds can be spent

15. In government budgeting, there is a procedure known as *allotment*. 15.____
Of the following statements which relate to allotment, select the one that is MOST generally considered to be correct.
Allotment
A. increases the practice of budget units coming back to the legislature branch for supplemental appropriations
B. is simply an example of red tape
C. eliminates the requirement of timing of expenditures
D. is designed to prevent waste

16. In government budgeting, the establishment of the schedules of allotments is MOST generally the responsibility of the 16.____
A. budget unit and the legislature
B. budget unit and the executive
C. budget unit only
D. executive and the legislature

17. Of the following statements relating to preparation of an organization's budget request, which is the MOST generally valid precaution? 17.____
A. Give specific instructions on the format or budget requests and required supporting data
B. Because of the complexity of preparing a budget request, avoid argumentation to support the requests
C. Put requests in whatever format is desirable
D. Consider that final approval will be given to initial estimates

18. Of the following statements which relate to the budget process in a well-organized government, select the one that is MOST NEARLY correct. 18.____
A. The budget cycle is the step-by-step process which is repeated each and every fiscal year.
B. Securing approval of the budget does not take place within the budget cycle.

C. The development of a new budget and putting it into effect is a two-step process known as the budget cycle.
D. The fiscal period, usually a fiscal year, has no relation to the budget cycle.

19. If a manager were asked what PPBS stands for, he would be RIGHT if he said _____ budgeting system. 19.____
A. public planning
B. planning programming
C. planning projections
D. programming procedures

Questions 20-21.

DIRECTIONS: Questions 20 and 21 are to be answered on the basis of the following information.

Sample Budget

Refuse Collection	Amount
Personal Services	$30,000
Contractual Services	5,000
Supplies and Materials	5,000
Capital Outlay	10,000
	$50,000

Residential Collections	
Dwellings – 1 pickup per week	1,000
Tons of refuse collected per year	375
Cost of collections per ton	$ 8
Cost per dwelling pickup per year	$ 3
Total annual cost	$3,000

20. The sample budget shown is a simplified example of a _____ budget. 20.____
A. factorial B. performance C. qualitative D. rational

21. The budget shown in the sample differs CHIEFLY from line-item and program budgets in that it includes 21.____
A. objects of expenditure but not activities or functions
B. only activities, functions, and control
C. activities and functions but not objects of expenditures
D. levels of service

Question 22.

DIRECTIONS: Question 22 is to be answered on the basis of the following information.

Sample Budget

Environmental Safety		
Air Pollution Protection		
Personal Services	$20,000,000	
Contractual Services	4,000,000	
Supplies and Materials	4,000,000	
Capital Outlay	2,000,000	
Total Air Pollution Protection		$30,000,000
Water Pollution Protection		
Personal Services	$23,000,000	
Supplies and Materials	4,500,000	
Capital Outlay	20,500,000	
Total Water Pollution Protection		$48,000,000
Total Environmental Safety		$78,000,000

22. Based on the above budget, which is the MOST valid statement? 22.____
    A. Environmental Safety, Air Pollution Protection, and Water Pollution Protection could all be considered program elements.
    B. The object listings included water pollution protection and capital outlay.
    C. Examples of the program element listings in the above are personal services and supplies and materials
    D. Contractual Services and Environmental Safety were the program element listings.

23. Which of the following is NOT an advantage of a program budget over a line-item budget? 23.____
    A program budget
    A. allows us to set up priority lists in deciding what activities we will spend our money on
    B. gives us more control over expenditures than a line-item budget
    C. is more informative in that we know the broad purposes of spending money
    D. enables us to see if one program is getting much less money than the others

24. If a manager were trying to explain the fundamental difference between traditional accounting theory and practice and the newer practice of managerial accounting, he would be MOST accurate if he said that 24.____
    A. traditional accounting practice focused on providing information for persons outside organizations, while managerial accounting focuses on providing information for people inside organizations
    B. traditional accounting practice focused on providing information for persons inside organizations while managerial accounting focuses on providing information for persons outside organizations

C. managerial accounting is exclusively concerned with historical facts while traditional accounting stresses future projections exclusively
D. traditional accounting practice is more budget-focused than managerial accounting

25. Which of the following formulas is used to determine the number of days required to process work? 25.____
_____ = Days to Process Work

A. $\frac{\text{Employees x Daily Output}}{\text{Volume}}$
B. $\frac{\text{Volume x Daily Output}}{\text{Volume}}$
C. $\frac{\text{Volume}}{\text{Employees x Daily Output}}$
D. $\frac{\text{Employees x Volume}}{\text{Daily Output}}$

KEY (CORRECT ANSWERS)

1.	C	11.	C
2.	C	12.	D
3.	D	13.	A
4.	B	14.	C
5.	D	15.	D
6.	D	16.	C
7.	D	17.	A
8.	A	18.	A
9.	B	19.	B
10.	C	20.	B

21.	D
22.	A
23.	B
24.	A
25.	C

TEST 3

DIRECTIONS: Each question or incomplete statement is followed by several suggested answers or completions. Select the one that BEST answers the question or completes the statement. *PRINT THE LETTER OF THE CORRECT ANSWER IN THE SPACE AT THE RIGHT.*

1. Electronic data processing equipment can produce more information faster than can be generated by any other means. 1.____
In view of this, the MOST important problem faced by management at present is to
   A. keep computers fully occupied
   B. find enough computer personnel
   C. assimilate and properly evaluate the information
   D. obtain funds to establish appropriate information systems

2. A well-designed management information system ESSENTIALLY provides each executive and manager the information he needs for 2.____
   A. determining computer time requirements
   B. planning and measuring results
   C. drawing a new organization chart
   D. developing a new office layout

3. It is generally agreed that management policies should be periodically reappraised and restated in accordance with current conditions. 3.____
Of the following, the approach which would be MOST effective in determining whether a policy should be revised is to
   A. conduct interviews with staff members at all levels in order to ascertain the relationship between the policy and actual practice
   B. make proposed revisions in the policy and apply it to current problems
   C. make up hypothetical situations using both the old policy and a revised version in order to make comparisons
   D. call a meeting of top level staff in order to discuss ways of revising the policy

4. Every manager has many occasions to lead a conference or participate in a conference of some sort. 4.____
Of the following statements that pertain to conferences and conference leadership, which is generally considered to be MOST valid?
   A. Since World War II, the trend has been toward fewer shared decisions and more conferences.
   B. The most important part of a conference leader's job is to direct discussion.
   C. In providing opportunities for group interaction, management should avoid consideration of its past management philosophy.
   D. A good administrator cannot lead a good conference if he is a poor public speaker.

5. Of the following, it is usually LEAST desirable for a conference leader to 5.____
   A. turn the question to the person who asked it
   B. summarize proceedings periodically
   C. make a practice of not repeating questions
   D. ask a question without indicating who is to reply

6. The behavioral school of management thought bases its beliefs on certain assumptions. 6.____
   Which of the following is NOT a belief of this school of thought?
   A. People tend to seek and accept responsibility.
   B. Most people can be creative in solving problems.
   C. People prefer security above all else.
   D. Commitment is the most important factor in motivating people.

7. The one of the following objectives which would be LEAST appropriate as a major goal of research in the field of human resources management is to 7.____
   A. predict future conditions, events, and manpower needs
   B. evaluate established policies, programs, and practices
   C. evaluate proposed policies, programs, and practices
   D. identify deficient organizational units and apply suitable penalties

8. Of the following general interviewing methods or techniques, the one that is USUALLY considered to be effective in counseling, grievances, and appraisal interviews is the _____ interview. 8.____
   A. directed B. non-directed C. panel D. patterned

9. The ESSENTIAL first phase of decision-making is 9.____
   A. finding alternative solutions
   B. making a diagnosis of the problem
   C. selecting the plan to follow
   D. analyzing and comparing alternative solutions

10. Assume that, in a certain organization, a situation has developed in which there is little difference in status or authority between individuals. 10.____
    Which of the following would be the MOST likely result with regard to communication in this organization?
    A. Both the accuracy and flow of communication will be improved.
    B. Both the accuracy and flow of communication will substantially decrease.
    C. Employees will seek more formal lines of communication.
    D. Neither the flow nor the accuracy of communication will be improved over the former hierarchical structure.

11. The main function of many agency administrative offices is *information management*. Information that is received by an administrative officer may be classified as active or passive, depending upon whether or not it requires the recipient to take some action. 11.____

Of the following, the item received which is clearly the MOST active information is
A. an appointment of a new staff member
B. a payment voucher for a new desk
C. a press release concerning a past city event
D. the minutes of a staff meeting

12. Which one of the following sets BEST describes the general order in which to teach an operation to a new employee? 12.____
A. Prepare, present, tryout, follow-up
B. Prepare, test, tryout, re-test
C. Present, test, tryout, follow-up
D. Test, present, follow-up, re-test

13. Of the following, public employees may be separated from public service 13.____
A. for the same reasons which are generally acceptable for discharging employees in private industry
B. only under the most trying circumstances
C. under procedures that are neither formalized nor subject to review
D. solely in extreme cases involving offenses of gravest character

14. Of the following, the one LEAST considered to be a communication barrier is 14.____
A. group feedback
B. charged words
C. selective perception
D. symbolic meanings

15. Of the following ways for a manager to handle his appointments, the BEST way, according to experts in administration, generally is to 15.____
A. schedule his own appointments and inform his secretary not to reserve his time without his approval
B. encourage everyone to make appointments through his secretary and tell her when he makes his own appointments
C. see no one who has not made a previous appointment
D. permit anyone to see him without an appointment

16. Assume that a manager decides to examine closely one of five units under his supervision to uncover problems common to all five. 16.____
His research technique is MOST closely related to the method called
A. experimentation
B. simulation
C. linear analysis
D. sampling

17. If one views the process of management as a dynamic process, which one of the following functions is NOT a legitimate part of that process? 17.____
A. Communication
B. Decision-making
C. Organizational slack
D. Motivation

18. Which of the following would be the BEST statement of a budget-oriented purpose for a government administrator? To 18.____
    A. provide 200 hours of instruction in basic reading for 3,500 adult illiterates at a cost of $1 million in the next fiscal year
    B. inform the public of adult educational programs
    C. facilitate the transfer to a city agency of certain functions of a federally-funded program which is being phased out
    D. improve the reading skills of the adult citizens in the city

19. Modern management philosophy and practices are changing to accommodate the expectations and motivations of organization personnel. 19.____
    Which of the following terms INCORRECTLY describes these newer managerial approaches?
    A. Rational management
    B. Participative management
    C. Decentralization
    D. Democratic supervision

20. Management studies support the hypothesis that, in spite of the tendency of employees to censor the information communicated to their supervisor, subordinates are MORE likely to communicate problem-oriented information upward when they have 20.____
    A. a long period of service in the organization
    B. a high degree of trust in the supervisor
    C. a high educational level
    D. low status on the organizational ladder

KEY (CORRECT ANSWERS)

1.	C	11.	A
2.	B	12.	A
3.	A	13.	A
4.	B	14.	A
5.	A	15.	B
6.	C	16.	D
7.	D	17.	C
8.	B	18.	A
9.	B	19.	A
10.	D	20.	B

EXAMINATION SECTION

TEST 1

DIRECTIONS: Each question or incomplete statement is followed by several suggested answers or completions. Select the one that BEST answers the question or completes the statement. *PRINT THE LETTER OF THE CORRECT ANSWER IN THE SPACE AT THE RIGHT.*

1. A management approach widely used today is based on the belief that decisions should be made and actions should be taken by managers closest to the organization's problems. 1.____
This style of management is MOST appropriately called _____ management.
   A. scientific
   B. means-end
   C. decentralized
   D. internal process

2. As contrasted with tall organization structures with narrow spans of control, flat organization structures with wide spans of control MOST usually provide 2.____
   A. fast communication and information flows
   B. more levels in the organizational hierarchy
   C. fewer workers reporting to supervisors
   D. lower motivation because of tighter control standards

3. Use of the systems approach is MOST likely to lead to 3.____
   A. consideration of the impact on the whole organization of actions taken in any part of that organization
   B. the placing of restrictions on departmental activity
   C. use of mathematical models to suboptimize production
   D. consideration of the activities of each unit of an organization as a totality without regard to the remainder of the organization

4. An administrator, with overall responsibility for all administrative operations in a large operating agency, is considering organizing the agency's personnel office around either of the following two alternative concepts: 4.____
Alternative I: A corps of specialists for each branch of personnel subject matter, whose skills, counsel, or work products are coordinated only by the agency personnel officer
Alternative II: A crew of so-called *personnel generalists*, who individually work with particular segments of the organization but deal with all subspecialties of the personnel function
The one of the following which MOST tends to be a DRAWBACK of Alternative I, as compared with Alternative II, is that
   A. training and employee relations work call for education, interests, and talents that differ from those required for classification and compensation work
   B. personnel office staff may develop only superficial familiarity with the specialized areas to which they have been assigned

C. supervisors may fail to get continuing overall personnel advice on an integrated basis
D. the personnel specialists are likely to become so interested in and identified with the operating view as to particular cases that they lose their professional objectivity and become merely advocates of what some supervisor wants

5. The matrix summary or decision matrix is a useful tool for making choices. Its effectiveness is MOST dependent upon the user's ability to 5.____
A. write a computer program (Fortran or Cobol)
B. assign weights representing the relative importance of the objectives
C. solve a set of two equations with two unknowns
D. work with matrix algebra

6. An organizational form which is set up only on an *ad hoc* basis to meet specific goals is said PRIMARILY to use 6.____
A. clean break departmentation
B. matrix or task force organization
C. scalar specialization
D. geographic or area-wide decentralization

7. The concept of job enlargement would LEAST properly be implemented by 7.____
A. permitting workers to follow through on tasks or projects from start to finish
B. delegating the maximum authority possible for decision-making to lower levels in the hierarchy
C. maximizing the number of professional classes in the classification plan
D. training employees to grow beyond whatever tasks they have been performing

8. As used in the area of admission, the principle of *unity of command* MOST specifically means that 8.____
A. an individual should report to only one superior for any single activity
B. individuals make better decisions than do committees
C. in large organizations, chains of command are normally too long
D. an individual should not supervise over five subordinates

9. The method of operations research, statistical decision-making, and linear programming have been referred to as the tool kit of the manager. Utilization of these tools is LEAST useful in the performance of which of the following functions? 9.____
A. Elimination of the need for using judgment when making decisions
B. Facilitation of decision-making without the need for sub-optimization
C. Quantifying problems for management study
D. Research and analysis of management operations

10. When acting in their respective managerial capacities, the chief executive officer and the office supervisor both perform the fundamental functions of management. 10.____
Of the following differences between the two, the one which is generally considered to be the LEAST significant is the
A. breadth of the objectives
B. complexity of measuring actual efficiency of performance
C. number of decisions made
D. organizational relationships affected by actions taken

11. The ability of operations researchers to solve complicated problems rests on their use of models. 11.____
These models can BEST be described as
A. mathematical statements of the problem
B. physical constructs that simulate a work layout
C. toy-like representations of employees in work environments
D. role-playing simulations

12. Of the following, it is MOST likely to be proper for the agency head to allow the agency personnel officer to make final selection of appointees from certified eligible lists where there are 12.____
A. *small* numbers of employees to be hired in newly-developed professional fields
B. *large* numbers of persons to be hired for key managerial positions
C. *large* numbers of persons to be hired in very routine occupations where the individual discretion of operating officials is not vital
D. *small* numbers of persons to be hired in highly specialized professional occupations which are vital to the agency's operations

13. Of the following, an operating agency personnel office is LEAST likely to be able to exert strong influence or control within the operating agency by 13.____
A. interpreting to the operating agency head what is intended by the directives and rules emanating from the central personnel agency
B. establishing the key objectives of those line divisions of the operating agency employing large numbers of staff and operating under the management-by-objectives approach
C. formulating and proposing to the agency head the internal policies and procedures on personnel matters required within the operating agency
D. exercising certain discretionary authority in the application of the agency head's general personnel policies to actual specific situations

14. PERT is a recently developed system used PRIMARILY to 14.____
A. evaluate the quality of applicants' background
B. analyze and control the timing aspects of a major project
C. control the total expenditure of agency funds within a monthly or quarterly time period
D. analyze and control the differential effect on costs of purchasing different quantities

15. Assume that an operating agency has among its vacant positions two positions, each of which encompasses mixed duties. Both require appointees to have considerable education and experience, but these requirements are essential only for the more difficult duties of these positions. In the place of these positions, an administrator creates two new positions, one in which the higher duties are concentrated and the other with the lesser functions requiring only minimum preparation. 15.____
Of the following, it is generally MOST appropriate to characterize the administrator's action as a(n)
A. *undesirable* example of deliberate downgrading of standards and requirements
B. *undesirable* manipulation of the classification system for non-merit purposes
C. *desirable* broadening of the definition of a class of positions
D. *desirable* example of job redesign

16. Of the following, the LEAST important stumbling block to the development of personnel mobility among governmental jurisdictions is the 16.____
A. limitations on lateral entry above junior levels in many jurisdictions
B. continued collection of filing fees for civil service tests by many governmental jurisdictions
C. absence of reciprocal exchange of retirement benefit eligibility between governments
D. disparities in salary scales between governments

17. Of the following, the MAJOR disadvantage of a personnel system that features the *selection out* (forced retirement) of those who have been passed over a number of times for promotion is that such a system 17.____
A. wastes manpower which is perfectly competent at one level but unable to rise above that level
B. wastes funds by requiring review boards
C. leads to excessive recruiting of newcomers from outside the system
D. may not be utilized in *closed* career systems with low maximum age limits for entrance

18. Of the following, the fields in which operating agency personnel offices generally exercise the MOST stringent controls over first line supervisors in the agency are 18.____
A. methods analysis and work simplification
B. selection and position classification
C. vestibule training and Gantt chart
D. suggestion systems and staff development

19. Of the following, computers are normally MOST effective in handling 19.____
A. large masses of data requiring simple processing
B. small amounts of data requiring constantly changing complex processing
C. data for which reported values are often subject to inaccuracies
D. large amounts of data requiring continual programming and reprocessing

20. Contingency planning, which has long been used by the military and is assuming increasing importance in other organizations, may BEST be described as a process which utilizes 20.____
   A. alternative plans based on varying assumptions
   B. *crash programs* by organizations departmentalized along process lines
   C. plans which mandate substitution of equipment for manpower at predetermined operational levels
   D. plans that individually and accurately predict future events

21. In the management of inventory, two kinds of costs normally determine when to order and in what amounts. 21.____
The one of the following choices which includes BOTH of these kinds of costs is _____ costs and _____ costs.
   A. carrying; storage
   B. personnel; order
   C. computer; order
   D. personnel; computer

22. At top management levels, the one of the following which is generally the MOST important executive skill is skill in 22.____
   A. budgeting procedures
   B. a technical discipline
   C. controlling actions in accordance with previously approved plans
   D. seeing the organization as a whole

23. Of the following, the BEST way to facilitate the successful operation of a committee is to set guidelines establishing its 23.____
   A. budget exclusive of personnel costs
   B. location
   C. schedule of meetings or conferences
   D. scope of purpose

24. Executive training programs that single out particular managers and groom them for promotion create the so-called organizational *crown princes*. 24.____
Of the following, the MOST serious problem that arises in connection with this practice is that
   A. the managers chosen for promotion seldom turn out to be the best managers since the future potential of persons cannot be predicted
   B. not enough effort is made to remove organizational obstacles in the way of their development and achievement
   C. the resentment of the managers not selected for the program has an adverse effect on the motivation of those managers not selected
   D. performance appraisal and review are not carried out systematically enough

25. Of the following, the LEAST likely result of the use of the concept of job enlargement is that 25.____
   A. coordination will be simplified
   B. the individual's job will become less challenging
   C. worker satisfaction will increase
   D. fewer people will have to give attention to each piece of work

KEY (CORRECT ANSWERS)

1. C
2. A
3. A
4. C
5. B

6. B
7. C
8. A
9. A
10. C

11. A
12. C
13. B
14. B
15. D

16. B
17. A
18. B
19. A
20. A

21. A
22. D
23. D
24. C
25. B

TEST 2

DIRECTIONS: Each question or incomplete statement is followed by several suggested answers or completions. Select the one that BEST answers the question or completes the statement. *PRINT THE LETTER OF THE CORRECT ANSWER IN THE SPACE AT THE RIGHT.*

1. The one of the following which is MOST likely to be emphasized in the use of the brainstorming technique is the 1.____
   A. early consideration of cost factors of all ideas which may be suggested
   B. avoidance of impractical suggestions
   C. separation of the generation of ideas from their evaluation
   D. appraisal of suggestions concurrently with their initial presentation

2. Of the following, the BEST method for assessing managerial performance is generally to 2.____
   A. compare the manager's accomplishments against clear, specific, agreed-upon goals
   B. compare the manager's traits with those of his peers on a predetermined objective
   C. measure the manager's behavior against a listing of itemized personal traits
   D. measure the manager's success according to the enumeration of the *satisfaction* principle

3. As compared with recruitment from outside, selection from within the service must generally show GREATER concern for the 3.____
   A. prestige in which the public service as a whole is held by the public
   B. morale of the candidate group compromising the recruitment field
   C. cost of examining per candidate
   D. benefits of the use of standardized and validated tests

4. Performance budgeting focuses PRIMARY attention upon which one of the following? The 4.____
   A. things to be acquired, such as supplies and equipment
   B. general character and relative importance of the work to be done or the service to be rendered
   C. list of personnel to be employed, by specific title
   D. separation of employee performance evaluations from employee compensation

5. Of the following, the FIRST step in the installation and operation of a performance budgeting system generally should be the 5.____
   A. identification of program costs in relationship to the accounting system and operating structure
   B. identification of the specific end results of past programs in other jurisdictions

C. identification of work programs that are meaningful for management purposes
D. establishment of organizational structures each containing only one work program

6. Of the following, the MOST important purpose of a system of quarterly allotments of appropriated funds generally is to enable the 6.____
A. head of the judicial branch to determine the legality of agency requests for budget increases
B. operating agencies of government to upgrade the quality of their services without increasing costs
C. head of the executive branch to control the rate at which the operating agencies obligate and expend funds
D. operating agencies of government to avoid payment for services which have not been properly rendered by employees

7. In the preparation of the agency's budget, the agency's central budget office has two responsibilities: program review and management improvement. Which one of the following questions concerning an operating agency's program is MOST closely related to the agency budget officer's program review responsibility? 7.____
A. Can expenditures for supplies, materials, or equipment be reduced?
B. Will improved work methods contribute to a more effective program?
C. What is the relative importance of this program as compared to a higher level of program performance?
D. Will a realignment of responsibilities contribute to a higher level of program performance?

8. Of the following, the method of evaluating relative rates of return normally and generally thought to be MOST useful in evaluating government operations is ______ analysis. 8.____
A. cost-benefit
B. budget variance
C. investment capital
D. budget planning program

9. The one of the following assumptions that is LEAST likely to be made by a democratic or permissive type of leader is that 9.____
A. commitment to goals is seldom a result of monetary rewards alone
B. people can learn not only to accept, but also to seek, responsibility
C. the average person prefers security over advancement
D. creativity may be found in most segments of the population

10. In attempting to motivate subordinates, a manager should PRINCIPALLY be aware of the fact that 10.____
A. the psychological qualities of people, in general, are easily predictable
B. fear, as a traditional form of motivation, has lost much of its former power to motivate people in our modern industrial society
C. fear is still the most potent force in motivating the behavior of subordinates in the public service
D. the worker has very little control over the quality and quantity of his output

11. Assume that the following figures represent the number of work-unit that were produced during a week by each of sixteen employees in a division: 11.____

12	16	13	18
21	12	16	13
16	13	17	21
13	15	18	20

If all of the employees of the division who produced thirteen work-units during the week had instead produced fifteen work-units during that same week, then for that week the
   A. mean, median, and mode would all change
   B. mean and mode would change, but the median would remain the same
   C. mode and median would change, but the mean would remain the same
   D. mode, mean, and median would all still remain unchanged in value

12. An important law in motivation theory is called the *law of effect*. This law says that behavior which satisfies a person's needs tends to be repeated; behavior which does not satisfy a person's needs tends to be eliminated. 12.____
The one of the following which is the BEST interpretation of this law is that
   A. productivity depends on personality traits
   B. diversity of goals leads to instability and motivation
   C. the greater the satisfaction, the more likely it is that the behavior will be reinforced
   D. extrinsic satisfaction is more important than intrinsic reward

13. Of the following, the MOST acceptable reason an administrator can give for taking advice from other employees in the organization only when he asks for it is that he wants to 13.____
   A. encourage creativity and high morale
   B. keep dysfunctional pressures and inconsistent recommendations to a minimum
   C. show his superiors and peers who is in charge
   D. show his subordinates who is in charge

14. A complete picture of the communication channels in an organization can BEST be revealed by 14.____
   A. observing the planned paperwork system
   B. recording the highly intermittent patterns of communication
   C. plotting the entire flow of information over a period of time
   D. monitoring the *grapevine*

Questions 15-16.

DIRECTIONS: Questions 15 and 16 are to be answered SOLELY on the basis of the following passage.

Management by objectives (MBO) may be defined as the process by which the superior and the subordinate managers of an organization jointly define its common goals, define each individual's major areas of responsibility in terms of the results expected of him and use these measures as guides for operating the unit and assessing the contribution of each of its members.

The MBO approach requires that after organizational goals are established and communicated, targets must be set for each individual position which are congruent with organizational goals. Periodic performance reviews and a final review using the objectives set as criteria are also basic to this approach.

Recent studies have shown that MBO programs are influenced by attitudes and perceptions of the boss, the company, the reward-punishment system, and the program itself. In addition, the manner in which the MBO program is carried out can influence the success of the program. A study done in the late sixties indicates that the best results are obtained when the manager sets goals which deal with significant problem areas in the organizational unit, or with the subordinate's personal deficiencies. These goals must be clear with regard to what is expected of the subordinate. The frequency of feedback is also important in the success of a management-by-objectives program. Generally, the greater the amount of feedback, the more successful the MBO program.

15. According to the above passage, the expected output for individual employees should be determined 15.____
    A. after a number of reviews of work performance
    B. after common organizational goals are defined
    C. before common organizational goals are defined
    D. on the basis of an employee's personal qualities

16. According to the above passage, the management-by-objectives approach requires 16.____
    A. less feedback than other types of management programs
    B. little review of on-the-job performance after the initial setting of goals
    C. general conformance between individual goals and organizational goals
    D. the setting of goals which deal with minor problem area in the organization

Questions 17-19.

DIRECTIONS: Questions 17 through 19 are to be answered SOLELY on the basis of the following passage.

During the last decade, a great deal of interest has been generated around the phenomenon of organizational development, or the process of developing human resources through conscious organization effort. Organizational development (OD) stresses improving interpersonal relationships and organizational skills, such as communication, to a much greater degree than individual training ever did.

The kind of training that an organization should emphasize depends upon the present and future structure of the organization. If future organizations are to be unstable, shifting coalitions, then individual skills and abilities, particularly those emphasizing innovativeness, creativity, flexibility, and the latest technological knowledge, are crucial, and individual training is most appropriate.

But if there is to be little change in organizational structure, then the main thrust of training should be group-oriented or organizational development. This approach seems better designed for overcoming hierarchical barriers, for developing a degree of interpersonal relationships which make communication along the chain of command possible, and for retaining a modicum of innovation and/or flexibility.

17. According to the above passage, group-oriented training is MOST useful in 17.____
    A. developing a communications system that will facilitate understanding through the chain of command
    B. highly flexible and mobile organizations
    C. preventing the crossing of hierarchical barriers within an organization
    D. saving energy otherwise wasted on developing methods of dealing with rigid hierarchies

18. The one of the following conclusions which can be drawn MOST appropriately from the above passage is that 18.____
    A. behavioral research supports the use of organizational development training method rather than individualized training
    B. it is easier to provide individualized training in specific skills than to set up sensitivity training programs
    C. organizational development eliminates innovative or flexible activity
    D. the nature of an organization greatly influences which training methods will be most effective

19. According to the above passage, the one of the following which is LEAST important for large-scale organizations geared to rapid and abrupt change is 19.____
    A. current technological information
    B. development of a high degree of interpersonal relationships
    C. development of individual skills and abilities
    D. emphasis on creativity

Questions 20-25.

DIRECTIONS: Each of Questions 20 through 25 consist of a statement which contains one word that is incorrectly used because it is not in keeping with the meaning that the quotation is evidently intended to convey. Determine which word is INCORRECTLY used. Select from the choices lettered A, B, C, and D the word which, when substituted for the incorrectly used word, would BEST help to convey the meaning of the statement.

20. One of the considerations likely to affect the currency of classification, particularly in professional and managerial occupations, is the impact of the incumbent's capacities on the job. Some work is highly susceptible to change as the result of the special talents or interests of the classifier. Organization should never be so rigid as not to capitalize on the innovative or unusual proclivities of its key employees. While a machine operator may not be able, even subtly, to change the character or level of his job, the design engineer, the attorney, or the organization and methods analyst might readily do so. Reliance on his judgment and the scope of his assignments may both grow as the result of his skill, insight, and capacity. 20.____
    A. unlikely B. incumbent C. directly D. scope

21. The supply of services by the state is not governed by market price. The aim is to supply such services to all who need them and to treat all consumers equally. This objective especially compels the civil servant to maintain a role f strict impartiality, based on the principle of equality of individual citizens vis-à-vis their government. However, there is a clear difference between being neutral and impartial. If the requirement is construed to mean that all civil servants should be political eunuchs, devoid of the drive and motivation essential to dynamic administration, then the concept of impartiality is being seriously utilized. Modern governments should not be stopped from demanding that their hirelings have not only the technical but the emotional qualifications necessary for whole-hearted effort. 21.____
    A. determined B. rule C. stable D. misapplied

22. The manager was barely listening. Recently, at the divisional level, several new fronts of troubles had erupted, including a requirement to increase production yet hold down operating costs and somehow raise quality standards. Though the three objectives were basically obsolete, top departmental management was insisting on the simultaneous attainment of them, an insistence not helping the manager's ulcer, an old enemy within. Thus, the manager could not find time for interest in individuals—only in statistics which regiment of individuals, like unconsidered Army privates, added up to. 22.____
    A. quantity B. battalion C. incompatible D. quiet

23. When a large volume of data flows directly between operators and first-line supervisors, senior executives tend to be out of the mainstream of work. Summary reports can increase their remoteness. An executive needs to know the volume, quality, and cost of completed work, and exceptional problems. In addition, he may desire information on key operating conditions. Summary reports on these matters are, therefore, essential features of a communications network and make delegation without loss of control possible. 23.____
    A. unimportant B. quantity C. offset D. incomplete

24. Of major significance in management is harmony between the overall objectives of the organization and the managerial objectives within that organization. In addition, harmony among goals of managers is impossible; they should not be at cross-purposes. Each manager's goal should supplement and assist the goals of his colleagues. Likewise, the objectives of individuals or non-management members should be harmonized with those of the manager. When this is accomplished, genuine teamwork is the result, and human relations are aided materially. The integration of managers' and individuals' goals aids in achieving greater work satisfaction at all levels. 24.____
A. competition B. dominate C. incremental D. vital

25. Change constantly challenges the manager. Some of this change is evolutionary, some revolutionary, some recognizable, some non-recognizable. Both forces within an enterprise and forces outside the enterprise cause managers to act and react in initiating changes in their immediate working environment. Change invalidates existing operations. Goals are not being accomplished in the best manner, problems develop, and frequently because of the lack of time, only patched-up solutions are followed. The result is that the mode of management is profound in nature and temporary in effectiveness. A complete overhaul of managerial operations should take place. It appears quite likely that we are just beginning to see the real effects of change in our society; the pace probably will accelerate in ways that few really understand or know how to handle. 25.____
A. confirms B. decline C. instituting D. superficial

KEY (CORRECT ANSWERS)

1. C
2. A
3. B
4. B
5. C

6. C
7. C
8. A
9. C
10. B

11. B
12. C
13. B
14. C
15. B

16. C
17. A
18. D
19. B
20. B

21. D
22. C
23. C
24. D
25. D

EXAMINATION SECTION

TEST 1

DIRECTIONS: Each question or incomplete statement is followed by several suggested answers or completions. Select the one that BEST answers the question or completes the statement. *PRINT THE LETTER OF THE CORRECT ANSWER IN THE SPACE AT THE RIGHT.*

1. Several employees complain informally to their supervisor regarding some new procedures which have been instituted. 1.____
The supervisor should IMMEDIATELY
   A. explain that management is responsible
   B. investigate the complaint
   C. refer the matter to the methods analyst
   D. tell the employees to submit their complaint as a formal grievance

2. The PRINCIPAL aim of an administrator is to 2.____
   A. act as liaison between employee and management
   B. get the work done
   C. keep up morale
   D. train his subordinates

3. Work measurement can be applied to operations where workload can be related to 3.____
   A. available personnel for the implementation of assigned tasks
   B. follow-up programs for continued progress
   C. cost abatement and optimum efficiency
   D. man hour utilization on assigned tasks

4. The one of the following which is NOT a primary advantage of a work measurement program is 4.____
   A. the selection of informed personnel
   B. knowledge of personnel needs
   C. support of personnel requests
   D. setting of approximate unit costs

5. A program of work measurement would be LEAST likely to 5.____
   A. point up the need for management research
   B. keep workload and personnel on an even keel
   C. measure the performance in exceptional operations
   D. evaluate the status of operations

6. Generally speaking, there are two kinds of work measurement: 6.____
(1) the traditional industrial engineering kind where performance standard are determined by time study or other engineering techniques, and (2) the statistical kind where yardsticks (so-called to distinguish them from engineered standard) are developed from a statistical analysis of past performance data. These data consist essentially of periodic reports in which work performed, expressed in identifiable work units, is related to the time required to perform it, usually expressed in man-hours.
The ESSENTIAL difference between the two kinds of work measurement is that
   A. the statistical type if based on past, current, and future determinants of a divergent nature, while engineered standards are restrictive
   B. yardsticks are less restrictive than engineered standards
   C. time study standards employ a higher ratio of man-hour data than do statistical standards
   D. engineered standards are more costly as well as more accurate than routine time study methods

7. Government has favored the use of the statistical type of work measurement over the industrial type MAINLY because 7.____
   A. government is an institution rarely hampered by money-seeking techniques
   B. as the statistical type of work measurement is broadly based, it is more capable of filling the wide expanse of government's needs
   C. employees might object vehemently against speed-ups, thereby sapping work measurement's force
   D. the former appears to be just as effective and less expensive than the latter

8. A work measurement program is a system by which a 8.____
   A. periodic account is kept of individual and group performance
   B. recurring account is kept of group performance
   C. periodic account is kept of performance by an individual
   D. periodic account is kept of performance by a group

9. Statistical standards developed during the early stages of a work measurement program are 9.____
   A. changed too rapidly and thus are of little value in the final program
   B. subject to change as the program moves forward
   C. incorporated into the final program, ultimately for research studies
   D. abandoned before the effective date of the final program

10. It is NOT an objective of a work measurement program to 10.____
   A. furnish a basis for procedural control
   B. provide a true basis for management control
   C. furnish a genuine basis for budget control
   D. provide a basis for management planning

11. The MOST valid of the following concepts of management control is that it examines 11.____
    A. the method with which work assignments have been accomplished in accordance with preconceived plans and policies
    B. preconceived plans and policies to determine their ultimate value
    C. results to determine how well work assignments have been accomplished in accordance with preconceived plans and policies
    D. the work of individual employees to get an acceptable, so as not to endanger the entire control program

12. Of the following, the LEAST likely area in which a deficiency in operations would be revealed by a work measurement program is 12.____
    A. improper personnel utilization
    B. inadequate equipment
    C. distribution of work
    D. personnel rating

13. The MOST accurate of the following statements regarding the standard as used in a work measurement program is: 13.____
    A. Standard rates of performance should not be established until the effectiveness of an operation has been determined.
    B. The measure of effectiveness should be kept separate and distinct from the application of standards to actual performance
    C. standards should not be used as guides in planning
    D. Standard rates of performance must be established before effectiveness of an operation can be determined.

14. The first and most important basic consideration in instituting a program of work measurement is the 14.____
    A. indoctrination of personnel
    B. establishment of a uniform technology
    C. selection of the time unit
    D. selection of a standard

15. A _____ is an item or a group of items, generally physical, which, when taken in the aggregate, serve to measure amounts of work. 15.____
    A. Therblig
    B. function
    C. operation
    D. work unit

16. Which of the following epitomizes the *raison d'etre* of work simplification? 16.____
    A. Waste elimination
    B. Empirical costs
    C. Time study speed-ups
    D. Charting techniques

17. A process charting analysis is likely to be of little value in the event of 17.____
    A. a major change in the department's activity
    B. a new supervisor from the outside coming in to head the unit
    C. increase in volume of work
    D. sizable personnel turnover

18. Staff or functional supervision in an organization 18.____
    A. is least justified at the operational level
    B. is contrary to the principle of Unity of Command
    C. is more effective than authoritative supervision
    D. normally does not give the right to take direct disciplinary action

19. The correlation between a flow process chart and a flow diagram is BEST described by which of the following statements? 19.____
    A. A flow process chart is supportive machinery to the flow diagram.
    B. In essence, the flow process chart exhibits time, distance, and location using standard symbols, whereas the flow diagram exhibits flow lines and uses classification symbols.
    C. Much of the information on the flow process chart is reproduced from the flow diagram.
    D. The flow diagram is complementary to the flow process chart.

20. Indicate which of the following statements is LEAST apt to clarify the underlying distinction between work simplification and other method of betterment procedures. 20.____
    Work simplification
    A. is dependent on supervisory participation
    B. is designed for employee participation
    C. emphasizes group participation
    D. emphasizes the ideas of experts

21. In describing the process of administrative management, the LEAST valid description is that it 21.____
    A. is composed of interdependent functions
    B. is comprised of related parts
    C. is cyclical
    D. consists of independent parts

22. Work activity, as to type, individual performance, and time expenditure, is BEST illustrated by a _____ chart. 22.____
    A. flow process
    B work flow
    C. work distribution
    D. operations

23. Neither the work distribution nor the flow process chart furnishes adequate intelligence as to 23.____
    A. methods
    B. activities
    C. nature of work activity
    D. unit prices

24. A graphic presentation of the steps and distribution through which each copy of a multiple copy office form travels is a(n) 24.____
    A. work distribution chart
    B. flow process chart
    C. flow diagram
    D. operations chart

25. A CHIEF target of work simplification is 25.____
    A. the achievement of greater productivity with the same effort
    B. obtaining the same work accomplishment with less effort
    C. employee participation and little resistance to change
    D. all of the above

KEY (CORRECT ANSWERS)

1.	B	11.	C
2.	B	12.	D
3.	D	13.	D
4.	A	14.	B
5.	C	15.	D
6.	B	16.	A
7.	D	17.	B
8.	B	18.	D
9.	B	19.	D
10.	A	20.	D

21.	D
22.	C
23.	D
24.	C
25.	C

TEST 2

DIRECTIONS: Each question or incomplete statement is followed by several suggested answers or completions. Select the one that BEST answers the question or completes the statement. *PRINT THE LETTER OF THE CORRECT ANSWER IN THE SPACE AT THE RIGHT.*

1. In conducting a work simplification program, which of the following office problems is the MOST likely to be solved by the use of the flow process chart? 1.____
   A. Are the employee deluged with unrelated tasks?
   B. What activities are the most costly, in terms of time consumed?
   C. Is the proper sequence of work activity employed?
   D. Is there an even distribution of work among the employees?

2. In the matter of procedural analysis, which question should be asked FIRST? 2.____
   A. When should the step be performed?
   B. Who should perform the step?
   C. What is the significance of the step?
   D. Where can this be improved upon?

3. Storage on a movement diagram is represented by 3.____
   A. ◇ B. ▽ C. □ D. all of the above

4. The use of a flow process chart is LESS desirable in indicating 4.____
   A. the time rate for each step B. distance traveled
   C. equipment-facilities layout D. sequence of activities

5. Division of work is BEST delineated by means of a _____ chart. 5.____
   A. work methods B. flow process
   C. work distribution D. flow authority

6. In seeking to conduct a work simplification analysis, the MOST appropriate first step would be to 6.____
   A. chart the procedures
   B. survey the facilities as to spatial access
   C. make problem area determination
   D. set up composition of forms analysis

7. The conception of a standard is BEST denoted as a 7.____
   A. hypothetical level B. circumscribed level of work activity
   C. level of comparing D. quintessential idea

8. With reference to office work simplification, it could be considered expedient to 8.____
   A. first simplify the procedure and then the individual methods
   B. simplify the individual methods first, then the procedure
   C. concurrently, simplify the methods and the procedure
   D. none of the above

9. The MOST valid precept relative to work analysis is 9.____
   A. the volume of work is inversely proportional to the distribution or sequence of work
   B. in meeting production standards, the sequence of work transcends its distribution
   C. work sequence and work distribution should be analyzed in relation to work volume
   D. work sequence and work distribution should be examined for work validation concepts

10. The flow process chart is PRINCIPALLY used 10.____
    A. as a useful tool to train new employees
    B. to ascertain the effectiveness of the organization's employees
    C. to pinpoint *bottlenecks* affecting an operation
    D. to determine the visibility of organizational relationships

11. The work distribution chart would generally be of little value in answering which of the following questions? 11.____
    A. In what order are the activities being carried out?
    B. Which activities consume the most time?
    C. Is a work balance maintained among the employees?
    D. Are the employees laboring under a plethora of unrelated tasks?

12. A worthwhile analytical tool in work simplification is the flow process chart. The MOST valid description is that 12.____
    A. a flow process chart is generally reliable without review for a period of a year
    B. the flow process chart should be reviewed and possibly revised at six-month intervals
    C. the flow process chart is an ad hoc instrument
    D. the value of a flow process chart is not determined by time

13. In the analysis of a method of procedure in a work simplification program, a competent analyst should FIRST focalize on the clearance or diminution of 13.____
    A. verifications
    B. transportations
    C. inspections
    D. storages

14. Which one of the following statements BEST distinguishes a method from a procedure? 14.____
    A. A method is a consistent sequence of procedures.
    B. A procedure comprises a sequence of related methods, performed in most instances by a single person.
    C. A series of related methods comprise a procedure.
    D. In breadth, a method takes precedence over a procedure.

15. The data provided by the flow process chart in a work simplification program is INADEQUATE to answer which one of the following questions? 15.____
    A. What is being performed?
    B. In what manner should the work be performed?
    C. What is the quantity of work performed?
    D. Who should perform the work?

Questions 16-17.

DIRECTIONS: Questions 16 and 17 are to be answered on the basis of the following passage.

Ideally, then, the process of budget formulation would consist of a flow of directives down the organization, and a reverse flow of recommendations in terms of alternatives among which selection would be made at every level. Ideally, also, a change in the recommendations at any level would require reconsideration and revision at all lower levels. By a process of successive approximation, everything would be taken into account and all points of view harmonized. Such a process, however, would be ideal only if the future could be foreseen clearly and time did not matter. As it is, in a complicated organization like the Federal government, the initial policy objectives established for the budget become out-of-date, before such a procedure could be carried through. While this difficulty does not in any way impugn the principle that the budget should be considered in terms of alternatives, it may call for short-cut methods of estimation rather than long drawn-out ones.

16. According to the above passage, 16.____
    A. the ideal method for estimating purposes is a short one
    B. the ideal method is not ideal for use in the Federal government
    C. directive should flow up and down via short methods
    D. the Federal government needs to speed up its reverse flow of recommendations for greater budgetary estimates

17. A suitable title for the above passage would be: 17.____
    A. Formulating the Federal Government's Budgetary Principles
    B. Directives and Recommendations: Budgetary Flow
    C. The Process of Budget Formulation
    D. The Application of the Ideal Estimate to the Federal Government

Questions 18-19.

DIRECTIONS: Questions 18 and 19 are to be answered on the basis of the following passage.

For purpose of budget formulation, the association of budgeting with accounting is less fortunate. Preparing for the future and recording the past do not necessarily require the same aptitudes or attitudes. The task of the accountant is to record past transactions in meticulous detail. Budgeting involves estimates of an uncertain future. But, because of the influence of accounts, government's budgets are prepared in a degree of detail that is quite unwarranted by the uncertain assumptions on which the estimates are based. A major source of government waste could be eliminated if estimates were prepared in no greater detail than was justified by their accuracy.

18. The author of the above paragraph 18.____
    A. is undermining the accounting profession
    B. believes accountants dwell solely in the past and cannot deal with the future efficiently
    C. wants the accountants out of government unless they become more accurate in their findings
    D. wishes to redirect the accountants' handling of budget procedures

19. The author's attitude appears to be 19.____
    A. tongue-in-cheek B morose
    C. strident D. constructive

20. The idea that classic organizational structure tends to create work situations having requirements counter to those for psychological success and self-esteem, sometimes called the *organizational dilemma*, is MOST closely associated with 20.____
    A. Argyris B. Taylor C. Gulick D. Maslow

Questions 21-25.

DIRECTIONS: Questions 21 through 25 contain incorrectly used words which change the meaning of the statement. Identify the word in the statement that is incorrect and select the choice that would make the sentence correct.

21. Standards of production performance are necessary to reveal the quantities of material, the number of hours of labor, the machine hours, and quantities of service (as, for example, power, steam, etc.) necessary to perform the various production operations. The establishment of such standards is an engineering rather than an accounting task, but it should be emphasized that such standards are needless to the development of the budgetary procedure—at least insofar as the budget is to serve as a tool of control. Such standards serve not only in the development of the budget and in measuring efficiency of production performance, but also in developing purchase requirements and in estimating costs. 21.____
    A. Manifest B. Evaluation C. Essential D. Function

22. Where standard costs are not available or their use is impracticable due to uncertainty of prices, estimates of the costs must be made on the basis of past experience and expected conditions. Ability to use standards largely eliminates the use of the budget for purposes of control of costs but its value remains for purposes of coordination of the program with purchases and finance. 22.____
    A. Failure B. Current C. Culmination D. Apparent

23. While one of the first objectives of the labor budget is to provide the highest practicable degree of regularity of employment, consideration must also be given to the estimating and perdurability of labor cost. Regularity of employment in itself effects some reduction in labor cost, but when carried beyond the point of practicality, it may increase other costs. For example, additional sales effort may be required to expand sales volume or to develop new products for slack periods; the cost of carrying inventories and the dangers of obsolescence and price declines must also be considered. A proper balance must be secured. 23.____
A. Material B. Control C. Futures D. To

24. The essentials of budgeting perhaps can be summarized in this manner: 24.____
I. Develop a sound business program
II. Report on the progress in achieving that program
III. Take necessary action as to all variances which are inevitable
IV. Revise the program to meet the changing conditions as required

A. Perfect B. Plans C. Controllable D. Secure

25. If a planning and control procedure is considered worthwhile, then it is a syllogism that preparation for the installation should be adequate. Time devoted to this educational aspect ordinarily will prove quite rewarding. The management to be involved with the budget, and particularly the middle management, must have a clear understanding of the budgetary procedure. 25.____
A. Acquired B. Remedial C. Monetary D. Truism

KEY (CORRECT ANSWERS)

1.	D	11.	A
2.	C	12.	D
3.	D	13.	D
4.	C	14.	C
5.	C	15.	C
6.	C	16.	B
7.	C	17.	C
8.	A	18.	D
9.	C	19.	D
10.	C	20.	A

21.	C
22.	B
23.	B
24.	C
25.	D

TEST 3

DIRECTIONS: Each question or incomplete statement is followed by several suggested answers or completions. Select the one that BEST answers the question or completes the statement. *PRINT THE LETTER OF THE CORRECT ANSWER IN THE SPACE AT THE RIGHT.*

1. The MOST important element in job satisfaction is 1.____
   A. job security
   B. responsibility or recognition
   C. salary
   D. type of supervision

2. The point of view that the average person wishes to avoid responsibility, wishes to be directed, as little ambition, and wants security above all, is described by Douglas MacGregor as Theory 2.____
   A. X
   B. Y
   C. Z
   D. X and Y combined

3. To prepare a work distribution chart, two other types of lists must generally be prepared. 3.____
   In usual order of preparation, they are a(n) _____ and a(n) _____ list.
   A. flow chart; activity
   B. skills list; task
   C. task list; activity
   D. activity list; task

4. A statistical control program in an office is valuable to direct deterioration in operations. 4.____
   It is, however, LEAST likely to reveal
   A. when preventative action is needed
   B. when a variation is due to chance
   C. when an assignable cause is present
   D. what the cause of error or deterioration is

5. Which of the following BEST defines an organization chart? 5.____
   An organizational chart
   A. depicts informal channels of communication within an organization
   B. depicts the major functions of an organization and the normal work flow between subdivisions of the organization
   C. presents graphically the arrangement and interrelationships of the subdivisions and the functions of the organization as they exist
   D. presents graphically the arrangement and relationships of all the positions authorized in an organization

6. In considering an office layout for a unit, which of the following factors should generally receive the LEAST consideration? 6.____
   A. Lighting levels in the existing area
   B. Major work flow—the processing of paper
   C. Present and projected growth rate of the unit
   D. Traffic patterns of employees and visitors

7. The BEST way to secure effective management is usually to 7.____
   A. allow staff to help solve administrative problems of line management
   B. provide a good organization structure
   C. select capable managers
   D. set up conservative spans of control

8. Which of the following is NOT an advantage of oral instruction as compared with written instructions? 8.____
   Oral
   A. instructions can be easily changed
   B. instructions are superior in transmitting complex directives
   C. instructions facilitate exchange of information between a supervisor and his subordinate(s)
   D. discussions are possible with oral instructions, making it easier to ascertain understanding

9. Which organization principle is MOST closely related to procedural analysis and improvement? 9.____
   A. Duplication, overlapping, and conflict should be eliminated.
   B. The objectives of the organization should be clearly defined.
   C. Managerial authority should be clearly defined.
   D. Top management should be freed of burdensome details.

10. Of the following control techniques, a _____ is MOST useful on large, complex projects. 10.____
    A. general work plan   B. Gantt chart
    C. monthly progress report   D. PERT chart

11. Work is organized so that the work is broken down into a series of jobs. Each unit of work moves progressively from position to position until completion. 11.____
    This paragraph BEST describes a
    A. parallel plan of work subdivision   B. serial plan
    C. unit assembly plan   D. unit process plan

12. According to the classic studies of Rensis Likert, the GREATEST factor making for good morale and increased productivity was having a 12.____
    A. good program of employee benefits and wage scales
    B. supervisor who gave his employees free rein after they were fully trained and did not interfere with them
    C. supervisor who was primarily interested in production
    D. supervisor who, while interested in production, was primarily *employee-centered*

13. The managerial grid shows two concerns and a range of interaction between them. 13.____
In this grid, the horizontal axis indicates a concern for _____ and the vertical axis indicates a concern for _____.
   A. production; people
   B. hierarchy; people
   C. organization; people
   D. people; costs

14. It has been decided to make a few important revisions in the methods and procedures of a particular work unit. 14.____
Of the following, which method of implementing these revisions would probably be the MOST desirable in terms of morale and of efficiency?
   A. Give all employees in unit individual instructions in the revised procedures and make sure each employee knows them before instructing the next
   B. Institute all revisions at once, followed by on-the-job training for all members of the work unit
   C. Introduce the revisions one at a time and accompany each revision with an orientation for employees
   D. Set up a training course for the employees which instructs them in all aspects of the revised procedures prior to their implementation

15. An operations research technique which would be employed to determine the optimum number of window clerks or interviewers to have in an agency serving the public would MOST likely be the use of 15.____
   A. line of balance
   B. queueing theory
   C. simulation
   D. work sampling

16. Douglas MacGregor's theory of human motivation classifies worker behavior into two distinct categories: Theory X and Theory Y. Theory X, the traditional view, states that the average man dislikes working and will avoid work if he can, unless coerced. Theory Y holds essentially the opposite view. 16.____
The manager can apply both of these theories to worker behavior BEST if he
   A. follows an *open-door* policy only with respect to his immediate subordinates
   B. recognizes his subordinates' mental and social needs as well as agency needs
   C. recognizes that executive responsibility is primarily limited to fulfillment of agency productivity goals
   D. directs his subordinate managers to follow a policy of close supervision

17. In interpersonal communications, it is important to ascertain whether oral directions and instruction are understood. 17.____
One of the MOST important sources of such information is known as
   A. the *halo* effect
   B. evaluation
   C. feedback
   D. quantitative analysis

18. The *grapevine* MOST often provides a useful service by 18.____
    A. correcting some of the deficiencies of the formal communication system
    B. rapidly conveying a true picture of events
    C. involving staff in current organizational changes
    D. interfering with the operation of the formal communication system

19. People who are in favor of a leadership style in which the subordinates help make decisions contend that it produces favorable effects in a work unit. According to these people, which of the following is NOT likely to be an effect of such *participative management*? 19.____
    A. Reduced turnover
    B. Accelerated learning of duties
    C. Greater acceptance of change
    D. Reduced appearance of the work unit's goals

20. Employees of a public service agency will be MOST likely to develop meaningful goals for both the agency and the employee and become committed to attaining them if supervisors 20.____
    A. allow them unilaterally to set their own goals
    B. provide them with a clear understanding of the premises underlying the agency's goals
    C. encourage them to concentrate on setting only short-range goals for themselves
    D. periodically review the agency's goals in order to suggest changes in accordance with current conditions

KEY (CORRECT ANSWERS)

1.	B	11.	B
2.	A	12.	D
3.	C	13.	A
4.	D	14.	D
5.	C	15.	B
6.	A	16.	B
7.	B	17.	C
8.	B	18.	A
9.	A	19.	D
10.	D	20.	B

EXAMINATION SECTION
TEST 1

DIRECTIONS: Each question or incomplete statement is followed by several suggested answers or completions. Select the one that BEST answers the question or completes the statement. *PRINT THE LETTER OF THE CORRECT ANSWER IN THE SPACE AT THE RIGHT.*

1. Which one of the following is LEAST likely to be an area or cause of trouble in the use of staff personnel? 1.______

   A. Misunderstanding of the role the staff personnel are supposed to play as a result of vagueness of definition of their duties and authority
   B. Tendency of staff personnel almost always to be older than line personnel at comparable salary levels with whom they must deal
   C. Selection of staff personnel who fail to have simultaneously both competence in their specialities and skill in staff work
   D. The staff person fails to understand mixed staff and operating duties

2. Which of the following is generally NOT a valid statement with respect to the supervisory process? 2.______

   A. General supervision is more effective than close supervision.
   B. Employee-centered supervisors lead more effectively than do production-centered supervisors.
   C. Employee satisfaction is directly related to productivity.
   D. Low-producing supervisors use techniques that are different from high-producing supervisors.

3. Which of the following is the MOST essential element for proper evaluation of the performance of subordinate supervisors? 3.______

   A. Careful definition of each supervisor's specific job responsibilities and of his progress in meeting mutually agreed upon work goals
   B. System of rewards and penalties based on each supervisor's progress in meeting clearly defined performance standards
   C. Definition of personality traits, such as industry, initiative, dependability, and cooperativeness, required for effective job performance
   D. Breakdown of each supervisor's job into separate components and a rating of his performance on each individual task

4. The PRINCIPAL advantage of specialization for the operating efficiency of a public service agency is that specialization 4.______

   A. reduces the amount of red tape in coordinating the activities of mutually dependent departments
   B. simplifies the problem of developing adequate job controls
   C. provides employees with a clear understanding of the relationship of their activities to the overall objectives of the agency
   D. reduces destructive competition for power between departments

5. A list of conditions which encourages good morale inside a work group would NOT include a 5.______

   A. high rate of agreement among group members on values and objectives
   B. tight control system to minimize the risk of individual error
   C. good possibility that joint action will accomplish goals
   D. past history of successful group accomplishment

6. Of the following, the MOST important factor to be considered in selecting a training strategy or program is the 6.______

   A. requirements of the job to be performed by the trainees
   B. educational level or prior training of the trainees
   C. size of the training group
   D. quality and competence of available training specialists

7. Of the following, the one which is considered to be LEAST characteristic of the higher ranks of management is 7.______

   A. that higher levels of management benefit from modern technology
   B. that success is measured by the extent to which objectives are achieved
   C. the number of subordinates that directly report to a manager
   D. the de-emphasis of individual and specialized performance

8. Assume that a manager is preparing a training syllabus to be used in training members of her staff. 8.______
   Which of the following would NOT be a valid principle of the learning process to consider when preparing this training syllabus?

   A. When a person has thoroughly learned a task, it takes a lot of effort to create a little more improvement.
   B. In complicated learning situations, there is a period in which an additional period of practice produces an equal amount of improvement in learning.
   C. The less a person knows about the task, the slower the initial progress.
   D. The more a person knows about the task, the slower the initial progress.

9. Which statement BEST illustrates when collective bargaining agreements are working well? 9.______

   A. Executives strongly support subordinate managers.
   B. The management rights clause in the contract is clear and enforced.
   C. Contract provisions are competently interpreted.
   D. The provisions of the agreement are properly interpreted, communicated, and observed.

10. An executive who wishes to encourage subordinates to communicate freely with him about a job-related problem should FIRST 10.______

A. state his own position on the problem before listening to the subordinates' ideas
B. invite subordinates to give their own opinions on the problem
C. ask subordinates for their reactions to his own ideas about the problem
D. guard the confidentiality of management information about the problem

11. The ability to deal constructively with intra-organizational conflict is an essential attribute of the successful manager. 11.______
The one of the following types of conflict which would be LEAST difficult to handle constructively is a situation in which there is

A. agreement on objectives, but disagreement as to the probable results of adopting the various alternatives
B. agreement on objectives, disagreement on alternative courses of action, and relative certainty as to the outcome of one of the alternatives
C. disagreement on objectives and on alternative courses of action, and relative certainty as to the outcome of one of the alternatives
D. disagreement on objectives and on alternative courses of action, but uncertainty as to the outcome of the alternatives

12. Which of the following actions does NOT belong in a properly conducted grievance handling process? 12.______

A. Gathering relevant information on why the grievance arose
B. Formulating a personal judgment about the fairness or unfairness of the grievance at the time the grievance is presented
C. Establishing tentative answers to the grievance
D. Following up to see whether the solution has eliminated the difficulty

13. Grievances are generally defined as complaints expressed over work-related matters. 13.______
Which one of the following is MOST important for managers to be aware of in connection with this definition?
The

A. fact that the definition fails to separate the subject of the grievance from the attitude of the grievant
B. fact that anything in the organization may be the source of the grievance
C. need to assume that dissatisfied people have adverse effects on productivity
D. implication that management should be concerned about expressed grievances and unconcerned about unexpressed grievances

14. In carrying out disciplinary action, the MOST important procedure for all managers to follow is to 14.______

A. convince all levels of management on the need for discipline from the organization's viewpoint
B. follow up on a disciplinary action and not assume that the action has been effective
C. convince all executives that proper discipline is a legitimate tool for their use
D. convince all executives that they need to display confidence in the organization's rules

15. Assume that an employee under your supervision is acquitted in court of criminal charges arising out of his employment. 15.______
Of the following statements concerning disciplinary action, which is MOST NEARLY correct?

A. Disciplinary proceedings against the employee may not be held for the same offenses on which he was tried and acquitted.
B. In a disciplinary action, the acquittal dispenses with the requirement that the employee be advised as to his constitutional rights.
C. Civil Rights Law Section 79 prohibits the taking of any further punitive action by an employer if the offense did not involve official corruption.
D. It is possible for the employee to be found guilty of the same offense when tried in a departmental hearing.

16. Work rules can be an effective tool in the process of personnel management. 16.______
The BEST practical definition for work rules is that they are

A. minimum standards of conduct or performance that apply to individuals or groups at work in an organization
B. prescriptions that serve to specialize employee behavior
C. predetermined decisions about disciplinary action
D. the major determinant of an organization's climate and the morale of its workforce

Questions 17-18

DIRECTIONS: Questions 17 and 18 pertain to identification of words that are incorrectly used because they are not in keeping with the meaning of the quotation. In answering each question, the first step is to read the passage and identify the incorrectly used word, and then select the word which, when substituted, BEST serves to convey the meaning of the quotation.

17. Among the Housing Manager's overall responsibilities in administering a project is the prevention of the development of conditions which might lead to termination of tenancy and eviction of a tenant. Where there appears to be doubt that a tenant is fully aware of his responsibilities and is thus jeopardizing his tenancy, the Housing Manager should acquaint him with these responsibilities. Where a situation involves behavior of a tenant or a member of his family, the Housing Manager should confirm, through discussions and referrals to social agencies, correction of the conditions before they reach a state where there is no alternative but termination proceedings. 17.______

A. Coordinate
B. Identify
C. Assert
D. Attempt

18. The one universal administrative complaint is that the budget is inadequate. Between adequacy and inadequacy lie all degrees of adequacy. Further, human wants are modest in relation to human resources. From these two facts we may conclude that the fundamental criterion of administrative decision must be a criterion of efficiency (the degree to which the goals have been reached relative to the available resources) rather than a criterion of adequacy (the degree to which its goals have been reached). The task of the manager is to maximize social values relative to limited resources. 18.______

A. Improve
B. Simple
C. Limitless
D. Optimize

Questions 19-21.

DIRECTIONS: Questions 19 through 21 are to be answered SOLELY on the basis of the following situation.

John Foley, a top administrator, is responsible for output in his organization. Because productivity had been lagging for two periods in a row, Foley decided to establish a committee of his subordinate managers to investigate the reasons for the poor performance and to make recommendations for improvements. After two meetings, the committee came to the conclusions and made the recommendations that follow.

Output forecasts had been handed down from the top without prior consultation with middle management and first level supervision. Lines of authority and responsibility had been unclear. The planning and control process should be decentralized.

After receiving the committee's recommendations, Foley proceeded to take the following actions. Foley decided he would retain final authority to establish quotas but would delegate to the middle managers the responsibility for meeting quotas.

After receiving Foley's decision, the middle managers proceeded to delegate to the first-line supervisors the authority to establish their own quotas. The middle managers eventually received and combined the first-line supervisors' quotas so that these conformed to Foley's.

19. Foley's decision to delegate responsibility for meeting quotas to the middle managers is inconsistent with sound management principles because 19.______

A. Foley should not have involved himself in the first place
B. middle managers do not have the necessary skills
C. quotas should be established by the chief executive
D. responsibility should not be delegated

20. The principle of co-extensiveness of responsibility and authority bears on Foley's decision. 20.______
In this case, it implies that

A. authority should exceed responsibility
B. authority should be delegated to match the degree of responsibility
C. both authority and responsibility should be retained and not delegated
D. responsibility should be delegated, but authority should be retained

21. The middle managers' decision to delegate to the first-line supervisors the authority to establish quotas was INCORRECTLY reasoned because 21.______

A. delegation and control must go together
B. first-line supervisors are in no position to establish quotas
C. one cannot delegate authority that one does not possess
D. the meeting of quotas should not be delegated

22. If one attempts to list the advantages of the management-by-exception principle as it is used in connection with the budgeting process, several distinct advantages could be cited. 22.______
Which of the following is NOT an advantage of this principle as it applies to the budgeting process?
Management-by-exception

A. saves time
B. identifies critical problem areas
C. focuses attention and concentrates effort
D. escalates the frequency and importance of budget-related decisions

23. The MOST accurate description of a budget is that 23.______

A. a budget is made up by an organization to plan its future activities
B. a budget specifies in dollars and cents how much is spent in a particular time period
C. a budget specifies how much the organization to which it relates estimates it will spend over a certain period of time
D. all plans dealing with money are budgets

24. Of the following, the one which is NOT a contribution that a budget makes to organizational programming is that a budget 24.______

A. enables a comparison of what actually happened with what was expected
B. stresses the need to forecast specific goals and eliminates the need to focus on tasks needed to accomplish goals
C. may illustrate duplication of effort between interdependent activities
D. shows the relationship between various organizational segments

25. A line-item budget is a good control budget because 25.______

A. it clearly specifies how the items being purchased will be used
B. expenditures can be shown primarily for contractual services
C. it clearly specifies what the money is buying
D. it clearly specifies the services to be provided

KEY (CORRECT ANSWERS)

1.	B	11.	B
2.	C	12.	B
3.	A	13.	C
4.	B	14.	B
5.	B	15.	D
6.	A	16.	A
7.	A	17.	D
8.	D	18.	C
9.	D	19.	D
10.	B	20.	B

21. C
22. D
23. C
24. B
25. C

TEST 2

DIRECTIONS: Each question or incomplete statement is followed by several suggested answers or completions. Select the one that BEST answers the question or completes the statement. *PRINT THE LETTER OF THE CORRECT ANSWER IN THE SPACE AT THE RIGHT.*

1. The insights of Chester I. Barnard have influenced the development of management thought in significant ways. He is MOST closely identified with a position that has become known as the 1.______

   A. acceptance theory of authority
   B. principle of the manager's or executive's span of control
   C. *Theory X* and *Theory Y* dichotomy
   D. unit of command principle

2. Certain conditions should exist to insure that a subordinate will decide to accept a communication as being authoritative. 2.______
   Which of the following is LEAST valid as a condition which should exist?

   A. The subordinate understands the communication.
   B. At the time of the subordinate's decision, he views the communication as consistent with the organization's purpose and his personal interest.
   C. At the time of the subordinate's decision, he views the communication as more consistent with his personal purposes than with the organization's interest.
   D. The subordinate is mentally and physically able to comply with the communication.

3. In exploring the effects that employee participation has on implementing changes in work methods, certain relationships have been established between participation and productivity. 3.______
   It has MOST generally been found that highest productivity occurs in groups provided with

   A. participation in the process of change only through representatives of their group
   B. no participation in the change process
   C. full participation in the change process
   D. intermittent participation in the process of change

4. The trend LEAST likely to occur in the area of employee-management relations is that 4.______

   A. employees will exert more influence on decisions affecting their interests
   B. technological change will have a stronger impact on organizations' human resources
   C. labor will judge management according to company profits
   D. government will play a larger role in balancing the interests of the parties in labor-management affairs

5. Members of an organization must satisfy several fundamental psychological needs in order to be happy and productive. The BROADEST and MOST basic needs are 5.______

A. achievement, recognition, and acceptance
B. competition, recognition, and accomplishment
C. salary increments and recognition
D. acceptance of competition and economic award

6. Morale has been defined as the capacity of a group of people to pull together steadily for a common purpose. Morale thus defined is MOST generally dependent on 6.______

A. job security
B. group and individual self-confidence
C. organizational efficiency
D. physical health of the individuals

7. Which is the CORRECT order of steps to follow when revising office procedure? To 7.______

I. develop the improved method as determined by time and motion studies and effective workplace layout
II. find out how the task is now performed
III. apply the new method
IV. analyze the current method

The CORRECT answer is:
A. IV, II, I, III
B. II, I, III, IV
C. I, II, IV, III
D. II, IV, I, III

8. In contrast to broad spans of control, narrow spans of control are MOST likely to 8.______

A. provide opportunity for more personal contact between superior and subordinate
B. encourage decentralization
C. stress individual initiative
D. foster group of team effort

9. A manager is coaching a subordinate on the nature of decision-making. She could BEST define decision-making as 9.______

A. choosing between alternatives
B. making diagnoses of feasible ends
C. making diagnoses of feasible means
D. comparing alternatives

10. Of the following, the LEAST valid purpose of an organizational policy statement is to 10.______

A. keep personnel from performing improper actions and functions on routine matters
B. prevent the mishandling of non-routine matters
C. provide management personnel with a tool that precludes the need for their use of judgment
D. provide standard decisions and approaches in handling problems of a recurrent nature

11. Current thinking on bureaucratic organizations is that 11.______

A. bureaucracy is on the way out
B. bureaucracy, though not perfect, is unlikely to be replaced
C. bureaucratic organizations are most effective in dealing with constant change
D. bureaucratic organizations are most effective when dealing with sophisticated customers or clients

12. The development of alternate plans as a major step in planning will normally result in the planner's having several possible course of action available. GENERALLY, this is 12.______

A. *desirable* since such development helps to determine the most suitable alternative and to provide for the unexpected
B. *desirable* since such development makes the use of planning premises and constraints unnecessary
C. *undesirable* since the planners should formulate only one way of achieving given goals at a given time
D. *undesirable* since such action restricts efforts to modify the planning to take advantage of opportunities

13. Assume a manager carries out his responsibilities to his staff according to what is now known about managerial leadership. 13.______
Which of the following statements would MOST accurately reflect his assumptions about proper management?

A. Efficiency in operations results from allowing the human element to participate in a minimal way.
B. Efficient operation results from balancing work considerations with personnel considerations.
C. Efficient operation results from a work force committed to its self-interest.
D. Efficient operation results from staff relationships that produce a friendly work climate.

14. Assume that a manager is called upon to conduct a management audit. To do this properly, he would have to take certain steps in a specific sequence. Which step should this manager take FIRST? 14.______

    A. Managerial performance must be surveyed.
    B. A method of reporting must be established.
    C. Management auditing procedures and documentation must be developed.
    D. Criteria for the audit must be established.

15. If a manager is required to conduct a scientific investigation of an organizational problem, the FIRST step he should take is to 15.______

    A. state his assumptions about the problem
    B. carry out a search for background information
    C. choose the right approach to investigate the validity of his assumptions
    D. define and state the problem

16. A manager would be correct to assert that the principle of delegation states that decisions should be made PRIMARILY 16.______

    A. by persons in an executive capacity qualified to make them
    B. by persons in a non-executive capacity
    C. at as low an organizational level of authority as practicable
    D. by the next lower level of authority

17. Of the following, which one is NOT regarded by management authorities as a fundamental characteristic of an ideal bureaucracy? 17.______

    A. Division of labor and specialization
    B. An established hierarchy
    C. Decentralization of authority
    D. A set of operating rules and regulations

18. As the number of subordinates in a manager's span of control increases, the actual number of possible relationships 18.______

    A. increases disproportionately to the number of subordinates
    B. increases in equal number to the number of subordinates
    C. reaches a stable level
    D. will first increase, then slowly decrease

19. Management experts generally believe that computer-based management information systems (MIS) have greater potential for improving the process of management than any other development in recent decades.
The one of the following which MOST accurately describes the objectives of MIS is to 19.______

A. provide information for decision-making on planning, initiating, and controlling the operations of the various units of the organization
B. establish mechanization of routine functions such as clerical records, payroll, inventory, and accounts receivable in order to promote economy and efficiency
C. computerize decision-making on planning, initiating, organizing, and controlling the operations of an organization
D. provide accurate facts and figures on the various programs of the organization to be used for purposes of planning and research

20. The one of the following which is the BEST application of the *management-by-exception* principle is that this principle 20.______

A. stimulates communication and aids in management of crisis situations, thus reducing the frequency of decision-making
B. saves time and reserves top management decisions only for crisis situations, thus reducing the frequency of decision-making
C. stimulates communication, saves time, and reduces the frequency of decision-making
D. is limited to crisis-management situations

21. Generally, each organization is dependent upon the availability of qualified personnel.
Of the following, the MOST important factor affecting the availability of qualified people to each organization is 21.______

A. availability of public transportation
B. the general rise in the educational levels of our population
C. the rise of sentiment against racial discrimination
D. pressure by organized community groups

22. A fundamental responsibility of all managers is to decide what physical facilities and equipment are needed to help attain basic goals.
Good planning for the purchase and use of equipment is seldom easy to do and is complicated most by the fact that 22.______

A. organizations rarely have stable sources of supply
B. nearly all managers tend to be better at personnel planning than at equipment planning
C. decisions concerning physical resources are made too often on an emergency basis rather than under carefully prepared policies
D. legal rulings relative to depreciation fluctuate very frequently

23. In attempting to reconcile managerial objectives and an individual employee's goals, it is generally LEAST desirable for management to 23.______

A. recognize the capacity of the individual to contribute toward realization of managerial goals
B. encourage self-development of the employee to exceed minimum job performance
C. consider an individual employee's work separately from other employees
D. demonstrate that an employee advances only to the extent that he contributes directly to the accomplishment of stated goals

24. As a management tool for discovering individual training needs, a job analysis would generally be of LEAST assistance in determining 24.______

A. the performance requirements of individual jobs
B. actual employee performance on the job
C. acceptable standards of performance
D. training needs for individual jobs

25. One of the major concerns of organizational managers today is how the spread of automation will affect them and the status of their positions. Realistically speaking, one can say that the MOST likely effect of our newer forms of highly automated technology on managers will be to 25.______

A. make most top-level positions superfluous or obsolete
B. reduce the importance of managerial work in general
C. replace the work of managers with the work of technicians
D. increase the importance of and demand for top managerial personnel

KEY (CORRECT ANSWERS)

1. A
2. C
3. C
4. C
5. A
6. B
7. D
8. A
9. A
10. C
11. B
12. A
13. B
14. D
15. D
16. C
17. C
18. A
19. A
20. C
21. B
22. C
23. C
24. B
25. D

EXAMINATION SECTION
TEST 1

DIRECTIONS: Each question or incomplete statement is followed by several suggested answers or completions. Select the one that BEST answers the question or completes the statement. *PRINT THE LETTER OF THE CORRECT ANSWER IN THE SPACE AT THE RIGHT.*

1. You are assigned to form a new unit to compile data which is to facilitate an executive in decision-making. 1.____
In planning the organization of this unit, the question to be answered FIRST is:

   A. What interpretations are likely to be made of the data by the executive in making a decision?
   B. At what point in the decision-making process will the data be most usefully introduced?
   C. What type of data is needed by the executive in his area of decision-making?
   D. What criteria will the executive use to evaluate the data?

2. The extent of effective decentralization within an organization is INVERSELY related to the 2.____

   A. size of the organization
   B. availability of sufficient competent personnel
   C. physical dispersion of the organization's activities
   D. effectiveness of communication within the organization

3. *The tasks of coordination, supervision, and control are likely to become more complicated as the specialization of an organization increases.* 3.____
This statement is GENERALLY

   A. *false;* better performance of these tasks is likely to follow from the detailed attention given to particular problems
   B. *false;* the proportion of specialized personnel is small in proportion to total personnel
   C. *true;* the increased interrelationships arising from increased specialization are sources of potential friction
   D. *true;* the specialist tends to resent direction from superiors who are not specialists

4. The distinctive feature between a method and a procedure may BEST be illustrated by a 4.____

   A. series of procedures comprising a method
   B. series of related methods performed usually by one person constituting a procedure
   C. procedure comprised of a series of related methods
   D. procedure encompassing a range more limited than that of a method

5. As part of your duties to analyze operating practices, you make a tour of a unit during which you talk to the employees about work methods, problems, and other pertinent topics. Such informal data gathering is often incomplete or inaccurate. At a later meeting with the unit supervisor, you question him about the information you have gathered, but he is unable to answer the questions immediately. He asks to accompany you on another tour of his unit and answer the questions on the spot. Explaining that employees will be reluctant to speak up in the presence of a supervisor, you refuse.
The situation you have created may BEST be described as a violation of the principle of organization called 5.____

A. delegation of authority
B. specialization of work
C. span of control
D. unity of command

6. A person desiring greater status and income in municipal government must, with few exceptions, move into the supervisory ranks. When he does, he will encounter certain changes in attitudes and relationships to which he must make satisfactory adjustments. His rise will create a degree of hostility and natural jealousy among his colleagues who have not tried to improve their situation or who have tried and failed. In a sense, too, he is forced upon the group he will supervise because under normal civil service practice, the group has little to say in his appointment.
A subtle change takes place also in his social situation; he must be in contact with his subordinates but he cannot be part of them, otherwise he yields a basic obligation to management, of which he is a part.
The MOST important conclusion to be made from this statement is that 6.____

A. a manager should limit his contacts with subordinates to a minimum
B. he must plan to advance himself further
C. he should isolate himself from the work of the supervised group
D. he must subordinate personnel popularity to the interest of the organization

7. A budget that itemizes expenditure estimates by detailing materials to be purchased, equipment to be maintained, salaries to be paid, etcetera, is known as a ______ budget. 7.____

A. performance
B. capital
C. line-item
D. program

8. Organizational activities for which there are no allocated funds available are financed from the ______ funds. 8.____

A. special revenue
B. sinking
C. general
D. special assessment

9. One of the real revolutions in public administration during the last half-century is the growth in importance of the budget as a planning and control instrument. Several trends account for this growing importance. Which of the following is NOT one of these trends? 9.____

A. Rapid growth of the urban population
B. The cheapening of the dollar
C. The improved standards of living
D. Full employment

10. The position classifying bureau of the personnel agency is normally NOT responsible for 10.____

A. allocating individuals to classes
B. assigning titles to classes of positions
C. establishing minimum qualifications for positions
D. determining which positions are necessary

11. Which of the following statements concerning a job analysis for position classification is FALSE? 11.____

A. It is a study of the person who is to occupy the job.
B. Time and motion studies may be used.
C. It may be used in establishing rates of compensation.
D. It is often done by staff authority.

12. Which of the following is considered to be an ESSENTIAL element of classifying a position? 12.____

A. Number of positions similar to the one being classified
B. Determination of salary to be paid for position
C. Comparison of the position with similar and related positions
D. Evaluation of the skills demanded by the position

13. The LEAST important objective of devising a service rating system is 13.____

A. validating selection procedures
B. improving quality of supervision
C. encouraging the development of employee performance
D. furnishing the basis of formulating a position classification plan

Questions 14-15.

DIRECTIONS: Questions 14 and 15 are to be answered in accordance with the following statement.

The process of validating a factual proposition is quite distinct from the process of validating a value judgment. The former is validated by its agreement with the facts, the latter by human authority.

14. According to the above statement, the one of the following methods which is MOST acceptable for determining whether or not a proposition is factually correct is to 14.____

A. prove that a related proposition is factually correct
B. derive it logically from accepted assumptions
C. show that it will lead to desired results
D. compare it with experience

15. Assuming that the above statement is correct, the theory that the correctness of all ethical propositions can be tested empirically is 15.____

A. *correct;* testing empirically is validating by agreement with facts
B. *incorrect;* ethical propositions are value judgments
C. *correct;* ethical propositions are based on rational hypotheses
D. *incorrect;* a factual proposition is validated by its agreement with facts

16. The rejection of the theory of inverse probability was, for a time, wrongly taken to imply that we cannot draw, from knowledge of a sample, inferences respecting the corresponding population. Such a view would entirely deny validity to all experimental science. According to the above statement, 16.____

A. the theory of inverse probability cannot be applied to an entire population
B. making deductions from a sample is consistent with experimental science
C. making deductions from a sample is inconsistent with experimental science
D. the theory of Inverse probability is based on the study of samples

17. May I point out that if technical employees are given assignments only in their special fields, there will be an immediate gain in conserving special skills. And, if we are to make optimum use of the abilities of the technical employees, it is necessary that these skills be conserved.
Assuming that this analysis is correct, it follows that 17.____

A. if we are not making optimum use of the abilities of technical employees, we have been giving technical employees assignments outside of their special fields
B. we are making optimum use of the abilities of technical employees if we conserve special skills
C. we are making optimum use of the abilities of technical employees if we give them assignments only in their special fields
D. we are not making optimum use of the abilities of technical employees if we give them assignments outside of their special fields

18. *It is less costly to replace old equipment than to repair it.*
Which of the following statements tends to prove this hypothesis MOST conclusively? 18.____

A. The repair of old equipment is frequently as costly as the purchase of new equipment.
B. Continuance in service of old equipment is at least as costly as its replacement by new equipment.
C. The replacement of old equipment is more desirable than its repair.
D. The cost for repairing old equipment is not a one-time cost, while the cost of new equipment is a one-time cost.

19. *An increasing birth rate will be followed by an increased school registration.*
On the basis of this statement *only*, it would be MOST accurate to state that 19.____

A. school registration does not change during a period with a level birth rate
B. an increasing school registration is preceded by a period with an increasing birth rate
C. a period with an increasing birth rate is sometimes followed by a decreasing school registration
D. a period with a decreasing birth rate is sometimes followed by a decreasing school registration

20. It is generally agreed that the *face-to-face* method of communicating is the most effective from a supervisor's standpoint. 20.____
This is true PRIMARILY because

A. the attitude of the recipient can be accurately appraised
B. it provides a two-way channel of expression which results in clarification of ideas
C. it is illustrative of the extremely desirable supervisory technique known as the *democratic approach*
D. it brings the supervisor closer to the actual level of operation

Questions 21-25.

DIRECTIONS: Questions 21 through 25 contain incorrectly used words which change the meaning of the statement. Identify the word in the statement that is incorrect and select the choice that would make the sentence correct.

21. Lack of employee input in the case of training often exists, but is frequently dealt with in evaluation of the training effort. Failure to deal with as important a factor as this can be ruinous to the training effort. 21.____

A. Seldom B. Margin C. Ancillary D. Contributory

22. It is a fallacy that policies generated at the top of the hierarchy are often not acceptable to those on the lower levels, particularly in the case of blue-collar workers among whom the rewards and sanctions of the union or members of the immediate social group are more impelling than the rewards or sanctions available to management. 22.____

A. Parologism
B. Truism
C. Commands
D. Undetermined

23. Basically, an organization develops when employees in it have rather free control over their behavior within the organization, when the philosophy of the organization is that maximum interpersonal interplay through a minimum number of hierarchical levels is desirable, and when a person traditionally called a *trainer* performs an integrating function. 23.____

A. Instinctively
B. Total
C. Flat
D. Strong

24. In gaining cooperation in human relations, the one who would influence must often foster his own ego and fertilize and feed that of the one who is to be influenced. 24.____

A. Lassitude B. Emulate C. Suppress D. Implant

25. In the United States, in general, we have been criticized for our emphasis upon physical, materialistic, and economic goals. These are still important, but the trends point toward the more complex, or appreciation of the beautiful, as for example in the architecture of our new factories and colors in the workplaces. 25.____

A. Ephemeral B. Concrete C. Prosaic D. Aesthetic

KEY (CORRECT ANSWERS)

1. C
2. D
3. C
4. C
5. D

6. D
7. C
8. C
9. D
10. D

11. A
12. C
13. D
14. D
15. B

16. B
17. D
18. B
19. B
20. B

21. A
22. B
23. D
24. C
25. D

TEST 2

DIRECTIONS: Each question or incomplete statement is followed by several suggested answers or completions. Select the one that BEST answers the question or completes the statement. *PRINT THE LETTER OF THE CORRECT ANSWER IN THE SPACE AT THE RIGHT.*

1. In the communications process, a formal communication should contain a multiplicity of ideas and several related objectives in order to provide for time-saving economy and to enhance the prospects of eventual compliance by subordinates. 1.____
This statement is GENERALLY

    A. *true,* since it reduces to a minimum the need for issuance of frequent communications from policy-making levels
    B. *false,* since the number of ideas and objectives contained in a single communication operates in inverse ratio to the degree of compliance
    C. *true,* since continuity and cohesiveness of plans are developed by infrequent but elaborate formal communications
    D. *false,* since time-saving devices are not the concern of superiors engaged in developing an effective communications process

2. Experts in supervisory practices have been emphasizing the importance of the art of listening on the part of supervisors. A recently published text devotes over three hundred pages to a discussion on how managers and supervisors can improve their ability to listen. 2.____
Which one of the following is NOT considered an important rule to follow in developing the skill of listening?

    A. Be attentive and concentrate on what is being said.
    B. Concentrate on the spoken word without concern for implied meanings.
    C. Ask an occasional question when appropriate to the discussion.
    D. Make sure you understand fully what is being said.

3. A supervisor who is to direct a team of senior clerks and clerks in a complex project calls them together beforehand to inform them of the tasks each employee will perform on this job. 3.____
Of the following, the CHIEF value of this action by the supervisor is that each member of this team will be able to

    A. work independently in the absence of the supervisor
    B. understand what he will do and how this will fit into the total picture
    C. share in the process of decision-making as an equal participant
    D. judge how well the plans for this assignment have been made

4. A supervisor who has both younger and older employees under his supervision may sometimes find that employee absenteeism seriously interferes with accomplishment of goals. 4.____
Studies of such employee absenteeism have shown that the absences of employees

    A. under 35 years of age are usually unexpected and the absences of employees over 45 years are usually unnecessary
    B. of all age groups show the same characteristics as to length of absence

C. under 35 years of age are for frequent, short periods while the absences of employees over 45 years of age are less frequent but of longer duration
D. under 35 years of age are for periods of long duration and the absences of employees over 45 years of age are for periods of short duration

5. A long-standing procedure for getting a certain job done by subordinates is apparently a good procedure. Changes in some steps of the procedure are made from time to time to handle special problems that come up. 5.____
Reviewing this procedure periodically is *desirable* MAINLY because

A. the system is working well
B. checking routines periodically is a supervisor"s chief responsibility
C. subordinates may be confused as to how the procedure operates as a result of the changes made
D. it is necessary to determine whether the procedure has become outdated or is in need of improvement

6. In conducting an interview, the BEST type of questions with which to begin the interview are those which the person interviewed is ______ to answer. 6.____

A. willing and able
B. willing but unable
C. able to, but unwilling
D. unable and unwilling

7. In order to determine accurately a child's age, it is BEST for an interviewer to rely on 7.____

A. the child's grade in school
B. what the mother says
C. birth records
D. a library card

8. In his first interview with a new employee, it would be LEAST appropriate for a unit supervisor to 8.____

A. find out the employee's preference for the several types of jobs to which he is able to assign him
B. determine whether the employee will make good promotion material
C. inform the employee of what his basic job responsibilities will be
D. inquire about the employee's education and previous employment

9. If an interviewer takes care to phrase his questions carefully and precisely, the result will MOST probably be that 9.____

A. he will be able to determine whether the person interviewed is being truthful
B. the free flow of the interview will be lost
C. he will get the information he wants
D. he will ask stereotyped questions and narrow the scope of the interview

10. During an interview, the person interviewed is LEAST likely to be cautious about what he tells the interviewer 10.____

A. shortly after the beginning when the questions normally suggest pleasant associations to the person interviewed
B. as long as the interviewer keeps the questions to the point

C. at the point where the person interviewed gains a clear insight into the area being discussed
D. when the interview appears formally ended and good-byes are being said

11. In an interview held for the purpose of getting information from the person interviewed, it is sometimes desirable for the interviewer to repeat the answer he has received to a question. 11.____
For the interviewer to rephrase such an answer in his own words is good practice MAINLY because it

A. gives the interviewer time to make up his next question
B. gives the person interviewed a chance to correct any possible misunderstanding
C. gives the person interviewed the feeling that the interviewer considers his answer important
D. prevents the person interviewed from changing his answer

12. There are several methods of formulating questions during an interview. The particular method used should be adapted to the interview problems presented by the person being questioned. 12.____
Of the following methods of formulating questions during an interview, the ACCEPTABLE one is for the interviewer to ask questions which

A. incorporate several items in order to allow a cooperative interviewee freedom to organize his statements
B. are ambiguous in order to foil a distrustful inter-viewee
C. suggest the correct answer in order to assist an interviewee who appears confused
D. would help an otherwise unresponsive interviewee to become more responsive

13. An interviewer permits the person being interviewed to read the data the interviewer writes as he records the person's responses on a routine departmental form. This practice is 13.____

A. *desirable,* because it serves to assure the person interviewed that his responses are being recorded accurately
B. *undesirable,* because it prevents the interviewer from clarifying uncertain points by asking additional questions
C. *desirable,* because it makes the time that the person interviewed must wait while the answer is written seem shorter
D. *undesirable,* because it destroys the confidentiality of the interview

14. Suppose that a stranger enters the office of which you are in charge and asks for the address and telephone number of one of your employees. 14.____
The MOST appropriate reaction would be to

A. find out why he needs the information and release it if his reason is a good one
B. explain that you are not permitted to release such information to unauthorized persons
C. give him the information but tell him it must be kept confidential
D. ask him to leave the office immediately

15. A member of the public approaches an employee who is at work at his desk. The employee cannot interrupt his work in order to take care of this person. The BEST and MOST courteous way of handling this situation is for the employee to 15.____

A. avoid looking up from his work until he is finished with what he is doing
B. tell this person that he will not be able to take care of him for quite a while
C. refer the individual to another employee who can take care of him right away
D. chat with the individual while he continues with his work

16. Some organizations, as a matter of policy, transfer their administrative staff personnel from one unit to another after stated periods of service in the unit. The MAIN advantage of such a policy is that it 16.____

A. helps keep the staff members abreast of the technical developments in their fields
B. impedes the formation of personal cliques among staff members
C. helps develop wider outlook and loyalty to the organization as a whole rather than to the unit assigned
D. permits the more effective utilization of the individual talents of staff members

17. Leaders generally are somewhat more intelligent than their followers. The CHIEF difficulty of the leader who is markedly more intelligent than his followers is that a leader has difficulty in 17.____

A. overcoming the suspicion and distrust of intellectuals on the part of the group
B. understanding the thought processes of persons who are intellectually inferior
C. accepting the irrational and emotional basis of much of human conduct
D. making himself understood by the group

18. A psychological study of leadership found that it is possible to predict the behavior of a new man in a leadership position more accurately on the basis of the behavior of his predecessor in the position than on the behavior of the man himself in his previous job. The BEST explanation of this observation is that there is a tendency 18.____

A. to select similar types of personalities to fill the same type of position
B. for a newly appointed man to avoid instituting basic changes in operational procedures
C. for a given organizational structure and set of duties to produce similar patterns of behavior
D. for increased responsibility to impose more mature patterns of behavior on an incumbent

19. An administrative official finds that the reports reaching him from his subordinates tend to exaggerate the favorable and minimize the unfavorable aspects of situations existing within the unit. The MOST valid conclusion to draw is that 19.____

A. the administrative official has been overly severe with subordinates and has instilled fear in them
B. there is a normal tendency for persons to represent themselves and their actions in the best possible light
C. members of the department tend to be optimists
D. the administrative official has not been sufficiently critical of previous reports and has not been alert to conditions in the unit

20. A special unit of a department is rife with rumors concerning plans for its future and the possibility of its abolition. As a result, morale and productivity of members assigned to it have suffered. To handle this situation, the administrative official in charge of the unit adopts a policy of promptly corroborating factual rumors and denying false ones. This method of dealing with the problem will achieve some good results, but its CHIEF weakness is that 20.____

A. it gives status to the rumors by the attention paid to them
B. the administrative official may not have the necessary information at hand to dispose promptly of all rumors
C. it *chases* the rumors rather than forestalling them by giving information concerning the unit's future
D. the administrative official may have confidential information which he should not divulge

21. An administrative official, realizing the importance of harmonious relationships within his unit, made a practice of unobtrusively intervening in any conflict situation between subordinates. Whenever friction seemed to be developing, he would attempt to soothe ruffled feelings, remove the source of difficulty by rescheduling activities or reassigning personnel,et cetera. His efforts were always behind-the-scenes and unknown to the employees involved. Although this method of operation produces some good results, its CHIEF drawback is that it 21.____

A. violates the chain of command principle
B. involves the administrative official in personal relationships which are not properly his concern
C. requires confidential sources of information about relationships within the unit, which borders on spying
D. permits subordinates to engage in unacceptable practices without correction

22. At a division conference at which a basic change in the department's procedure was to be announced, the conference leader started the discussion by asking the group for criticisms of the existing procedures. He then described the new procedures to be employed and explained the improvements in operations that were anticipated. The conference leader's method of introducing the change was 22.____

A. *good,* mainly because the conference members would be more receptive to the new procedure if they understood the inadequacies of the old
B. *bad,* mainly because the conference members would realize that the decision for change had been made before the discussion and without consideration of their comments
C. *good,* mainly because the comments and criticisms of the old procedure would provide the basis for evaluating the feasibility of the new method
D. *bad,* mainly because the focus of the discussion was on the procedure being replaced rather than on the procedure being introduced

23. A section chief in charge of a specialized unit calls a staff conference to discuss a proposed modification of some procedures. After making some introductory remarks, the chief wants the comments of the members of the staff. The staff consists of eight subordinates ranging in rank from office aide to principal administrative assistant III, each subordinate having responsibility for a different aspect of the program. Of the following, the BEST procedure for the chief to follow is to call upon each subordinate in 23.____

A. descending order of rank, mainly because the employees with the highest rank are likely to have the most experience and ability
B. ascending order of rank, mainly because the junior employees are more likely to be freer in their comments if they give their views before the senior employees speak
C. order of their specialized knowledge and competence in the subjects under discussion mainly because those with most knowledge and competence can best lead the discussion
D. order of seating around the table, mainly because informality of procedure and democrative leadership is obtained

24. As a supervisor assigned to a public relations unit in a city agency, you find a certain program under severe attack by a citizen's, group. 24.____
To be of GREATEST value to your supervisor, you should

A. present the department side of the story to all meetings or to all groups whether hostile or not
B. attempt to get another citizen's group to defend the department program
C. get greater support from the general public and the press to effectuate the program
D. ignore group opinions; rather, strive to affect individuals and let them persuade their groups

25. The commission has assigned you to present the department side to a group of citizens well-disposed to government programs. 25.____
You should present

A. *only* the department side
B. both sides of the story, but present the department side last
C. both sides of the story, but present the department side first
D. the facts and let the audience draw its own conclusion

KEY (CORRECT ANSWERS)

1. B
2. B
3. B
4. C
5. D

6. A
7. C
8. B
9. C
10. D

11. B
12. D
13. A
14. B
15. C

16. C
17. D
18. C
19. B
20. C

21. D
22. B
23. C
24. B
25. A

TEST 3

DIRECTIONS: Each question or incomplete statement is followed by several suggested answers or completions. Select the one that BEST answers the question or completes the statement. *PRINT THE LETTER OF THE CORRECT ANSWER IN THE SPACE AT THE RIGHT.*

1. Supervisor X, as a representative of the Commissioner, has been ordered to present the department arguments in reference to a new program of inspections and to emphasize such presentation by stressing the enforcement that will follow. 1.____
   In this instance,

   A. a mild threat is less of a deterrent than a strong threat
   B. any form of threat should be avoided since you are seeking cooperation
   C. an overly strong threat is less of a deterrent than a mild threat
   D. the mere statement that enforcement will follow is sufficient to effect cooperation

2. If, after an investigation and further consultation with central authorities, wholesale bribe-taking has been confirmed within a certain unit, the agency involved should 2.____

   A. withhold information from the public until a more secure image can be created
   B. break the story since such agency can present the least damaging picture
   C. arrange a compromise solution and present it to the public as an accomplished fact
   D. permit the central authorities to break the story since it presents a more efficient picture

3. The characteristic of flexibility versus stability of a policy seems contradictory to subordinate A. 3.____
   The difference can BEST be explained by the administrative manager if he points out that

   A. policies are decision guides and definite formulae for specific actions; therefore, stability must outweigh flexibility
   B. changing events and materials force a change in policy; therefore, flexibility refers to the ability to change policy when it becomes outmoded
   C. policy should be as stable as possible but sufficiently flexible to handle problems that vary from the normal; policy's true purpose must be understood as a guide for decisions, not an inflexible formula for action
   D. most policy at unit level is based on precedent and tradition and, therefore, subject always to the discretion of the supervisor

4. When an administrative manager devotes too much time to telling his subordinates how to handle their job problems, then he 4.____

   A. is spending too little time in formulating policies for the guidance of his subordinates
   B. is neglecting to delegate sufficient authority to his subordinates
   C. should immediately begin to plan for better use of his time
   D. should evaluate his approach to the administration of his section and establish better controls

5. Since the policies of a department are well established, an administrator does not need to formulate section policy. This statement is 5.____

   A. *true;* it is difficult for an administrator to establish a policy which will not in some way coincide or contradict established, overall policies
   B. *false;* department policies have to be broad enough to cover the whole organization; they are seldom detailed enough to guide a section in its internal organization
   C. *true;* the administrator's responsibility in this area is to formulate procedure to implement department policy
   D. *false;* uniformity of enforcement is essential, and this is impossible when the administrator does not establish his own section policy

6. Manager X, when giving a decision on a controversial item, reminds the subordinates of the policy under which such a decision was made.
   This reminder is 6.____

   A. *good;* the subordinates will be aware that he is not being arbitrary, operating by whim, or playing favorites
   B. *unnecessary;* policies have been explained over and over again to subordinates
   C. a form of buck-passing since the manager is blaming a policy for his unfavorable decision
   D. *bad;* policy commits management to specific decisions and, as such, should not be given unfavorable publicity

7. After objectives and policies have been stated, the next step should be to 7.____

   A. develop plans and procedures
   B. make forecasts
   C. examine conditions; gather data
   D. consider a budget

8. After establishing objectives and identifying problems and opportunities, the planning should be 8.____

   A. turned over to the controller. You can alter his plan if you do not agree.
   B. assigned to the division heads. Each will work out a plan for his own division
   C. a joint effort of the controller and other division heads. You and any staff experts available will cooperate and assist as planning progresses.
   D. a joint effort of all supervisors and subordinates

9. The MOST; accurate statement concerning plans and planning is: 9.____

   A. In the absence of an agency-wide plan, it is better to avoid planning in the individual work unit
   B. Every manager or supervisor must plan if he is to carry out his managerial functions
   C. Every manager should make a preliminary plan and then await the agency-wide plan
   D. The agency-wide plan should precede the preliminary plan

10. Objectives, programs, policies, budgets, and procedures are all ______ planning. 10.____

   A. elements of overall
   B. guides for
   C. alternates to
   D. methods of

11. Developing and understanding objectives, establishing policies, collecting data, developing alternative action proposals, and deciding on action are all 11.____

A. steps in planning
B. guidelines to consider in planning
C. the action motif ascribed to planning
D. alternatives to planning

12. Work measurement can be applied to operations where workload can be related to 12.____

A. available personnel for the implementation of assigned tasks
B. follow-up programs for continued progress
C. cost abatement and optimum efficiency
D. man-hour utilization on assigned tasks

13. If you ask for additional historical information on costs, caseloads, et cetera, you will be 13.____

A. refining the forecast process
B. developing the groundwork for forecasting
C. estimating the future
D. evaluating your research department's efficiency

14. Suppose that the majority of mathematical projections predicts a serious downturn in new cases, while you and your advisors believe that a mild upturn is approaching. In this situation, the BEST procedure is to 14.____

A. follow the course dictated by the mathematical projections because that is what they are there for
B. follow your own ideas and those of your advisors; management is an art, not a science
C. modify the course dictated by the mathematical projections so as to reflect both management and specialist judgment
D. consult another advisor

15. The director of a personnel bureau with 100 employees would probably operate MOST efficiently if he had under his immediate supervision approximately ______ subordinates. 15.____

A. 5 B. 25 C. 50 D. 100

16. A worker is *usually* MOST productive when he is assigned to work which 16.____

A. he is able to do best
B. involves a variety of skills
C. is under close supervision
D. requires little skill

17. It is desirable for all staff specialists to have some knowledge of line activities PRIMARILY in order that they may 17.____

A. direct line activities when necessary
B. have a proper framework for research
C. know how to deal with all types of personnel
D. take cognizance of the agency's needs and problems

18. When a supervisor delegates an assignment, he should 18.____

A. delegate his responsibility for the assignment
B. make certain that the assignment is properly performed
C. participate in the beginning and final stages of the assignment
D. retain all authority needed to complete the assignment

19. Which one of the following is LEAST important in the management of a suggestion program? 19.____

A. Giving awards which are of sufficient value to encourage competition
B. Securing full support from the department's officers and executives
C. Publicizing the program and the awards given
D. Providing suggestion boxes in numerous locations

20. The MOST certain means to *decrease* morale is to 20.____

A. insist on strict adherence to safety rules
B. make each employee responsible for the tidiness of his work area
C. overlook evidence of hostility between groups of employees
D. provide strong, aggressive leadership

KEY (CORRECT ANSWERS)

1.	C	11.	A
2.	B	12.	D
3.	C	13.	B
4.	A	14.	C
5.	B	15.	A
6.	A	16.	A
7.	C	17.	D
8.	C	18.	B
9.	B	19.	D
10.	A	20.	C

EXAMINATION SECTION

TEST 1

DIRECTIONS: Each question or incomplete statement is followed by several suggested answers or completions. Select the one that BEST answers the question or completes the statement. *PRINT THE LETTER OF THE CORRECT ANSWER IN THE SPACE AT THE RIGHT.*

1. In many instances, managers deliberately set up procedures and routines that more than one department or more than one employee is required to complete and verify an entire operation or transaction. 1.____
   The MAIN reason for establishing such routines is generally to
   A. minimize the chances of gaps and deficiencies in feedback of information to management
   B. expand the individual employee's vision and concern for broader organizational objectives
   C. provide satisfaction of employees' social and egoistic needs through teamwork and horizontal communications
   D. facilitate internal control designed to prevent errors, whether intentional or accidental

2. Committees—sometimes referred to as boards, commissions, or task forces—are widely used in government to investigate certain problems or to manage certain agencies. 2.____
   Of the following, the MOST serious limitation of the committee approach to management in government is that
   A. it reflects government's inability to delegate authority effectively to individual executives
   B. committee members do not usually have similar backgrounds, experience, and abilities
   C. it promotes horizontal communication at the expense of vertical communication
   D. the spreading out of responsibility to a committee often results in a willingness to settle for weak, compromise solutions

3. Of the following, the BEST reason for replacing methods of committees on a staggered or partial basis rather than replacing all members simultaneously is that this practice 3.____
   A. gives representatives of different interest groups a chance to contribute their ideas
   B. encourages continuity of policy since retained members are familiar with previous actions
   C. prevents the interpersonal frictions from building up and hindering the work of the group
   D. improves the quality of the group's recommendations and decisions by stimulating development of new ideas

4. Assume that in considering a variety of actions to take to solve a given problem, a manager decides to take no action at all. 4.____
According to generally accepted management practice, such a decision would be
   A. *proper*, because under normal circumstances it is better to make no decision
   B. *improper*, because inaction would be rightly construed as shunning one's responsibilities
   C. *proper*, since this would be a decision which might produce more positive results than the other alternatives
   D. *improper*, since such a solution would delay corrective action and exacerbate the problem

5. Some writers in the field of management assume that when a newly promoted manager has been informed by his superior about the subordinates he is to direct and the extent of his authority, that is all that is necessary. 5.____
However, thereafter, this new manager should realize that, for practical purposes, his authority will be effective ONLY when
   A. he accepts full responsibility for the actions of his subordinates
   B. his subordinates are motivated to carry out their assignments
   C. it derives from acceptable personal attributes rather than from his official position
   D. he exercises it in an authoritarian manner

6. A newly appointed manager is assigned to assist the head of a small developing agency handling innovative programs. Although this manager is a diligent worker, he does not delegate authority to middle- and lower-echelon supervisors. 6.____
The MOST important reason why it would be desirable to change this attitude toward delegation is because otherwise
   A. he may have to assume more responsibility for the actions of his subordinates than is implied in the authority delegated to him
   B. his subordinates will tend to produce innovative solutions on their own
   C. the agency will become a decentralized type of organization in which he cannot maintain adequate controls
   D. he may not have time to perform other essential tasks

7. All types of organizations and all functions within them are to varying degrees affected today by the need to understand the application of computer systems to management practices. 7.____
The one of the following purposes for which such systems would be MOST useful is to
   A. lower the costs of problem-solving by utilizing data that is already in the agency's control system correlated with new data
   B. stabilize basic patterns of the organization into long-term structures and relationships
   C. give instant solutions to complex problems
   D. affect savings in labor costs for office tasks involving non-routine complex problems

8. Compared to individual decision-making, group decision-making is burdened with the DISADVANTAGE of 8.____
   A. making snap judgments
   B. pressure to examine all relevant elements of the problem
   C. greater motivation needed to implement the decision
   D. the need to clarify problems for the group participants

9. Assume that a manager in an agency, faced with a major administrative problem, has developed a number of alternative solutions to the problem. 9.____
   Which of the following would be MOST effective in helping the manager make the best decision?
   A. *Experience*, because a manager can distill from the past the fundamental reasons for success or failure since the future generally duplicates the past
   B. *Experimentation*, because it is the method used in scientific inquiry and can be tried out economically in limited areas
   C. *Research analysis*, because it is generally less costly than most other methods and involves the interrelationships among the more critical factors that bear upon the goal sought
   D. *Value forecasting*, because it assigns numerical significance to the values of alternative tangible and intangible choices and indicates the degree of risk involved in each choice

10. Management information systems operate more effectively for managers than mere data tabulating systems because information systems 10.____
   A. eliminate the need for managers to tell information processors what is required
   B. are used primarily for staff rather than line functions
   C. are less expensive to operate than manual methods of data collection
   D. present and utilize data in a meaningful form

11. Project-type organizations are in widespread use today because they offer a number of advantages. 11.____
   The MOST important purpose of the project organization is to
   A. secure a higher degree of coordination than could be obtained in a conventional line structure
   B. provide an orderly way of phrasing projects in and out of organizations
   C. expedite routine administrative processes
   D. allow for rapid assessment of the status of any given project and its effect on agency productivity

12. A manager adjusts his plans for future activity by reviewing information about the performance of his subordinates. 12.____
   This is an application of the process of
   A. human factor impact
   B. coordinated response
   C. feedback communication
   D. reaction control

13. From the viewpoint of the manager in an agency, the one of the following which is the MOST constructive function of a status system or a rank system based on employee performance is that the system 13.____
   A. makes possible effective communication, thereby lessening social distances between organizational levels
   B. is helpful to employees of lesser ability because it provides them with an incentive to exceed their capacities
   C. encourages the employees to attain or exceed the goals set for them by the organization
   D. diminishes friction in assignment and work relationships of personnel

14. Some managers ask employees who have been newly hired by their agency and then assigned to their divisions or units such questions as: *What are your personal goals? What do you expect from your job? Why do you want to work for this organization?* 14.____
   For a manager to ask these questions is GENERALLY considered
   A. *inadvisable*; these questions should have been asked prior to hiring the employee
   B. *inadvisable*; the answers will arouse subjective prejudices in the manager before he sees what kind of work the employee can do
   C. *advisable*; this approach indicates to the employee that the manager is interested in him as an individual
   D. *advisable*; the manager can judge how much of a disparity exists between the employee's goals and the agency's goals

15. Assume that you have prepared a report to your superior recommending a reorganization of your staff to eliminate two levels of supervision. The total number of employees would remain the same, with the supervisors of the two eliminated levels taking on staff assignments. 15.____
   In your report, which one of the following should NOT be listed as an expected result of such a reorganization?
   A. Fewer breakdowns and distortions in communications to staff
   B. Greater need for training
   C. Broader opportunities for development of employee skills
   D. Fewer employee errors due to exercise of closer supervision and control

16. *Administration* has often been criticized as being unproductive in the sense that it seems far removed from the end products of an organization. 16.____
   According to modern management thought, this criticism, for the most part, is
   A. *invalid*, because administrators make it possible for subordinates to produce goods or services by directing coordination, and controlling their activities
   B. *valid*, because most subordinates usually do the work required to produce goods and services with only general direction from their immediate superiors
   C. *invalid*, because administrators must see to all of the details associated with the production of services
   D. *valid*, because administrators generally work behind the scenes and are mainly concerned with long-range planning

17. A manager must be able to evaluate the relative importance of his decisions and establish priorities for carrying them out. 17.____
Which one of the following factors bearing on the relative importance of making a decision would indicate to a manager that he can delegate that decision to a subordinate or give it low priority? The
   A. decision concerns a matter on which strict confidentiality must be maintained
   B. community impact of the decision is great
   C. decision can be easily changed
   D. decision commits the agency to heavy expenditure of funds

18. Suppose that you are responsible for reviewing and submitting to your superior the monthly reports from ten field auditors. Despite your repeated warnings to these auditors, most of them hand in their reports close to or after the deadline dates, so that you have no time to return them for revision and find yourself working overtime to make the necessary corrections yourself. The deadline dates for the auditors' reports and your report cannot be changed. 18.____
Of the following, the MOST probable cause for this continuing situation is that
   A. these auditors need retraining in the writing of this type of report
   B. possible disciplinary action as a result of the delay by the auditors has not been impressed upon them
   C. the auditors have had an opportunity to provide you with feedback to explain the reasons for the delays
   D. you, as the manager, have not used disciplinary measures of sufficient severity to change their behavior

19. Assume that an agency desiring to try out a *management-by-objectives* program has set down the guidelines listed below to implement this activity. Which one of these guidelines is MOST likely to present obstacles to the success of this type of program? 19.____
   A. Specific work objectives should be determined by top management for employees at all levels.
   B. Objectives should be specific, attainable, and preferably measurable as to units, costs, ratios, time, etc.
   C. Standards of performance should be either qualitative or quantitative, preferably quantitative.
   D. There should be recognition and rewards for successful achievement or objectives.

20. Of the following, the MOST meaningful way to express productivity where employees work a standard number of hours each day is in terms of the relationship between man- 20.____
   A. hours expended and number of work-units needed to produce the final product
   B. days expended and goods and services produced
   C. days and energy expended
   D. days expended and number of workers

21. Agencies often develop productivity indices for many of their activities. 21.____
Of the following, the MOST important use for such indices is generally to
   A. measure the agency's output against its own performance
   B. improve quality standards while letting productivity remain unchanged
   C. compare outputs of the agency with outputs in private industry
   D. determine manpower requirements

22. The MOST outstanding characteristic of staff authority, such as that of a public relations officer in an agency, as compared with line authority, is generally accepted to be 22.____
   A. reliance upon personal attributes
   B. direct relationship to the primary objectives of the organization
   C. absence of the right to direct or command
   D. responsibility for attention to technical details

23. In the traditional organization structure, there are often more barriers to upward communication than to downward communication. 23.____
From the viewpoint of a manager whose goal is to overcome obstacles to communication, this situation should be
   A. *accepted*; the downward system is the more important since it is highly directive, giving necessary orders, instructions, and procedures
   B. *changed*; the upward system should receive more emphasis than the downward system, which represents stifling bureaucratic authority
   C. *accepted*; it is generally conceded that upward systems supply enough feedback for control purposes necessary to the organization's survival
   D. *changed*; research has generally verified the need for an increase in upward communications to supply more information about employees' ideas, attitudes, and performance

24. A principal difficulty in productivity measurement for local government services is in defining and measuring output, a problem familiar to managers. A measurement that merely looks good, but which may be against the public interest, is another serious problem. Managers should avoid encouraging employees to take actions that lead to such measurements. 24.____
In accordance with the foregoing statement, it would be MOST desirable for a manager to develop a productivity measure that
   A. correlates the actual productivity measure with impact on benefit to the citizenry
   B. does not allow for a mandated annual increase in productivity
   C. firmly fixes priorities for resource allocations
   D. uses numerical output, by itself, in productivity incentive plans

25. For a manager, the MOST significant finding of the Hawthorne studies and experiments is that an employee's productivity is affected MOST favorably when the 25.____
   A. importance of tasks is emphasized and there is a logical arrangement of work functions

B. physical surroundings and work conditions are improved
C. organization has a good public relations program
D. employee is given recognition and allowed to participate in decision-making

KEY (CORRECT ANSWERS)

1.	D	11.	A
2.	D	12.	C
3.	B	13.	C
4.	C	14.	A
5.	B	15.	D
6.	D	16.	A
7.	A	17.	C
8.	D	18.	D
9.	C	19.	A
10.	D	20.	B
21.	A		
22.	C		
23.	D		
24.	A		
25.	D		

TEST 2

DIRECTIONS: Each question or incomplete statement is followed by several suggested answers or completions. Select the one that BEST answers the question or completes the statement. *PRINT THE LETTER OF THE CORRECT ANSWER IN THE SPACE AT THE RIGHT.*

1. Which one of the following is generally accepted by managers as the MOST difficult aspect of a training program in staff supervision? 1.____
   A. Determining training needs of the staff
   B. Evaluating the effectiveness of the courses
   C. Locating capable instructors to teach the courses
   D. Finding adequate space and scheduling acceptable times for all participants

2. Assume that, as a manager, you have decided to start a job enrichment program with the purpose of making jobs more varied and interesting in an effort to increase the motivation of a certain group of workers in your division. 2.____
   Which one of the following should generally NOT be part of this program?
   A. Increasing the accountability of these individuals for their own work
   B. Granting additional authority or job freedom to these employees in their job activities
   C. Mandating increased monthly production goals for this group of employees
   D. Giving each of these employees a complete unit of work

3. Both employer and employee have an important stake in effective preparation for retirement. 3.____
   According to modern management thinking, the one of the following which is probably the MOST important aspect of a sound pre-retirement program is to
   A. make assignments that utilize the employee's abilities fully
   B. reassign the employee to a less demanding position in the organization for the last year or two he is on the job
   C. provide the employee with financial data and other facts that would be pertinent to his retirement planning
   D. encourage the employee to develop interests and hobbies which are connected with the job

4. The civil service system generally emphasizes a policy of *promotion-from-within*. Employees in the direct line of promotion in a given occupational group are eligible for promotion to the next higher title in that occupational group. 4.____
   Which one of the following is LEAST likely to occur as a result of this policy and practice?
   A. Training time will be saved since employees in higher-level positions are already familiar with many agency rules, regulations, and procedures.
   B. The recruitment section will be able to show prospective employees that there are distinct promotional opportunities.

C. Employees will be provided with a clear-cut picture as to their possible career ladder.
D. Employees will be encouraged to seek broad-based training and education to enhance their promotability.

5. From a management point of view, the MAIAN drawback of seniority as opposed to merit as a basis for granting pay increases to workers is that a pay increase system based on seniority 5.____
A. is favored by unions
B. upsets organizational status relationships
C. may encourage mediocre performance by employees
D. is more difficult to administer than a merit plan

6. One of the actions that is often taken against employees in the non-uniformed forces who are accused of misconduct on the job is suspension without pay. 6.____
The MOST justifiable reason for taking such action is to
A. ease an employee out of the agency
B. enable an investigation to be conducted into the circumstances of the offense
C. improve the performance of the employee when he returns to the job
D. punish the employee by imposing a hardship on him

7. A manager has had difficulty in getting good clerical employees to staff a filing section under his supervision. To add to his problems, one of his most competent senior clerks requests a transfer to the accounting division so that he can utilize his new accounting skill, which he is acquiring by going to college at night. The manager attempts to keep the senior clerk in his filing section by calling the director of personnel and getting him to promise not to authorize any transfer. 7.____
GENERALLY, this manager's action is
A. *desirable*; he should not help his staff to develop themselves if it means losing good people
B. *undesirable*; he should recommend that the senior clerk get a raise in the hope of preventing him from transferring to another section
C. *desirable*; it shows that the manager is concerned about the senior clerk's future performance
D. *undesirable*; it is good policy to transfer employees to the type of work they are interested in and for which they are acquiring training

8. One of your subordinates, a unit supervisor, comes to you, the division chief, because he feels that he is working out of title, and he suggests that his competitive class position should be reclassified to a higher title. 8.____
Which one of the following statements that the subordinate has made is generally LEAST likely to be a valid support for his suggestion?
A. The work he is doing conforms to the general statement of duties and responsibilities as described in the class specification for the next higher title in his occupational group.
B. Most of the typical tasks he performs are listed in the class specification for a title with a higher salary range and are not listed for his current title.

C. His education and experience qualifications far exceed the minimum requirements for the position he holds.
D. His duties and responsibilities have changed recently and are now similar to those of his supervisor.

9. Assume that a class specification for a competitive title used exclusively by your agency is outdated, and that no examination for the title has been given since the specification was issued. 9.____
Of the following, the MOST appropriate action for your agency to take is to
A. make the necessary changes and submit the revised class specification to the city civil service commission
B. write the personnel director to recommend that the class specification be updated, giving the reasons and suggested revisions
C. prepare a revised class specification and submit it to the office of management and budget for their approval
D. secure approval of the state civil service commission to update the class specification, and then submit the revised specification to the city civil service commission

10. Assume that an appropriate eligible list has been established and certified to your agency for a title in which a large number of provisionals are serving in your agency. 10.____
In order to obtain permission from the personnel director to retain some of them beyond the usual time limit set by rules (two months) following certification of the list, which one of the following conditions MUST apply?
A. The positions are sensitive and require investigation of eligibles prior to appointment.
B. Replacement of all provisionals within two months would impair essential public service.
C. Employees are required to work rotating shifts, including nights and weekends.
D. The duties of the positions require unusual physical effort and endurance.

11. Under the federally-funded Comprehensive Employment and Training Act (CETA), the hiring by the city of non-civil servants for CETA jobs is PROHIBITED when the 11.____
A. applicants are unemployed because of seasonal lay-offs in private industry
B. applicants do not meet U.S. citizenship and city residence requirements
C. jobs have minimum requirements of specialized professional or technical training and experience
D. jobs are comparable to those performed by laid-off civil servants

12. Assume you are in charge of the duplicating service in your agency. Since employees assigned to this operation lack a sense of accomplishment because the work is highly specialized and repetitive, your superior proposes to enlarge the jobs of these workers and asks you about your reaction to this strategy. 12.____

The MOST appropriate response for you to make is that job enlargement would be

A. *undesirable*, primarily because it would increase production costs
B. *undesirable*, primarily because it would diminish the quality of the output
C. *desirable*, primarily because it might make it possible to add an entire level of management to the organizational structure of your agency
D. *desirable*, primarily because it might make it possible to decrease the amount of supervision the workers will require

13. According to civil service law, layoff or demotion must be made in inverse order of seniority among employees permanently serving in the same title and layoff unit. 13.____
Which one of the following is now the CORRECT formula for computing seniority?
Total continuous service in the

A. competitive class only
B. competitive, non-competitive, or labor class
C. classified or unclassified services
D. competitive, non-competitive, exempt, and labor classes

14. Under which of the following conditions would an appointing officer be permitted to consider the sex of a candidate in making an employment decision? 14.____
When

A. the duties of the position require considerable physical effort or strength
B. the duties of the position are considered inherently dangerous
C. separate toilet facilities and dressing rooms for the sexes are unavailable and/or cannot be provided in any event
D. the public has indicated a preference to be served by persons of a specified sex

15. Assume that an accountant under your supervision signs out to the field to make an agency audit. It is later discovered that, although he had reported himself at work until 5 P.M. that day, he had actually left for home at 3:30 P.M. Although this accountant has worked for the city for ten years and has had an excellent performance record, he is demoted to a lower title in punishment for this breach of duty. 15.____
According to generally accepted thinking on personnel management, the disciplinary action taken in this case should be considered

A. *appropriate*; a lesser penalty might encourage repetition of the offense
B. *inappropriate*; the correct penalty for such a breach of duty should be dismissal
C. *appropriate*; the accountant's abilities may be utilized better in the new assignment
D. *inappropriate*; the impact of a continuing stigma and loss of salary is not commensurate with the offense committed

16. Line managers often request more funds for their units than are actually required to attain their current objectives. 16.____
Which one of the following is the MOST important reason for such inflated budget requests?
The
   A. expectation that budget examiners will exercise their prerogative of budget cutting
   B. line manager's interest in improving the performance of his unit is thereby indicated to top management
   C. expectation that such requests will make it easier to obtain additional funds in future years
   D. opinion that it makes sense to obtain additional funds and decide later how to use them

17. Integrating budgeting with program planning and evaluation in a city agency is GENERALLY considered to be 17.____
   A. *undesirable*; budgeting must focus on the fiscal year at hand, whereas planning must concern itself with developments over a period of years
   B. *desirable*; budgeting facilitates the choice-making process by evaluating the financial implications of agency programs and forcing cost comparisons among them
   C. *undesirable*; accountants and statisticians with the required budgetary skills have little familiarity with the substantive programs that the agency is conducting
   D. *desirable*; such a partnership increases the budgetary skills of planners, thus promoting more effective use of public resources

18. An aspect of the managerial function, a budget is described BEST as a 18.____
   A. set of qualitative management controls over productivity
   B. tool based on historical accounting reports
   C. type of management plan expressed in quantitative terms
   D. precise estimate of future quantitative and qualitative contingencies

19. Which one of the following is generally accepted as the MAJOR immediate advantage of installing a system of program budgeting? 19.____
It
   A. encourages managers to relate their decisions to the agency's long-range goals
   B. is a replacement for the financial or fiscal budget
   C. decreases the need for managers to make trade-offs in the decision-making process
   D. helps to adjust budget figures to provide for unexpected developments

20. Of the following, the BEST means for assuring necessary responsiveness of a budgetary program to changing conditions is by 20.____
   A. overestimating budgetary expenditures by 15% and assigning the excess to unforeseen problem areas
   B. underestimating budgetary expenditures by at least 20% and setting aside a reserve account in the same amount

C. reviewing and revising the budget at regular intervals so that it retains its character as a current document
D. establishing *budget-by-exception* policies for each division in the agency

21. According to expert thought in the area of budgeting, participation in the preparation of a government agency's budget should GENERALLY involve 21.____
A. only top management
B. only lower levels of management
C. all levels of the organization
D. only a central budget office or bureau

22. Of the following, the MOST useful guide to analysis of budget estimates for the coming fiscal year is a comparison with 22.____
A. appropriations as amended for the current fiscal year
B. manpower requirements for the previous two years
C. initial appropriations for the current fiscal year
D. budget estimates for the preceding five years

23. A manager assigned to analyze the costs and benefits associated with a program which the agency head proposes to undertake may encounter certain factors which cannot be measured in dollar terms. 23.____
In such a case, the manager should GENERALLY
A. ignore the factors which cannot be quantified
B. evaluate the factors in accordance with their degree of importance to the overall agency goals
C. give the factors weight equal to the weight given to measurable costs and benefits
D. assume that non-measurable costs and benefits will balance out against one another

24. If city employees believe that they are receiving adverse treatment in terms of training and disciplinary actions because of their national origin, they may file charges of discrimination with the Federal government's 24.____
A. Human Rights Commission
B. Public Employee Relations Board
C. Equal Employment Opportunity Commission
D. United States Department of Commerce

25. Under existing employment statutes, the city is obligated, as an employer, to take *affirmative action* in certain instances. 25.____
This requirement has been imposed to ensure that
A. employees who are members of minority groups, or women, be given special opportunities for training and promotion even though they are not available to other employees
B. employees or applicants for employment are treated without regard to race, color, religion, sex, or national origin

C. proof exists to show that the city has acted with good intentions in any case where it has disregarded this requirement
D. men and women are treated alike except where State law provides special hour or working conditions for women

KEY (CORRECT ANSWERS)

1.	B	11.	D
2.	C	12.	D
3.	C	13.	D
4.	D	14.	C
5.	C	15.	D
6.	B	16.	A
7.	D	17.	B
8.	C	18.	C
9.	B	19.	A
10.	B	20.	D

21.	C
22.	A
23.	B
24.	C
25.	B

EXAMINATION SECTION

TEST 1

DIRECTIONS: Each question or incomplete statement is followed by several suggested answers or completions. Select the one that BEST answers the question or completes the statement. *PRINT THE LETTER OF THE CORRECT ANSWER IN THE SPACE AT THE RIGHT.*

1. Assume that a civil service list has been established for a position in an agency which had provisional appointees serving in three permanent vacancies. One of these provisionals is on the eligible list, but was discharged because permanent appointments were accepted by three eligibles who were higher on the list. The former provisional has complained to the agency head, alleging that special efforts were made to appoint these eligible. The personnel officer of the agency should advise the agency head that 1.____
   A. the court could compel them to appoint the former provisional appointee
   B. he is required by civil service law to appoint the higher ranking eligibles from the list
   C. the human rights commission could compel him to appoint the former provisional appointee
   D. he should attempt conciliation

2. Assume that two accountants working in a section under your supervision were appointed from the same eligible list. Accountant Jones received a higher score on the competitive examination than Accountant Doe; Jones was third on the eligible list and Doe was fifth. Jones was told to report to work on March 15 but Doe, who was working under a provisional appointment, was given permanent status as of March 1. For economic reasons, your agency head is considering abolishing one position of accountant and requests guidance from you before making any decision. 2.____
   It would be BEST to tell him that
   A. if he decides to abolish one position of accountant, he should lay off Jones because Doe was given permanent status before Jones
   B. under the rule of *one in three*, Doe could not have been reached for appointment before Jones, so that Doe would have to be laid off first
   C. if he decides to abolish one position of accountant, he should lay off Doe because Doe's provisional appointment was in violation of the Civil Service Law
   D. he should evaluate the performance of Jones and Doe before making any determination as to which accountant to lay off

3. An employee who has been on the job for a number of years became a problem drinker during the past year. The supervisor and this employee are good friends. 3.____
   Because this problem has been affecting the work of the unit adversely, it would be BEST for the supervisor to

A. attempt to cover up the problem by moving the subordinate's desk to a corner of the office where he would not be noticed so readily
B. refer the employee for counseling to the employee counseling service
C. reassign some of the problem drinker's responsibilities to other employees
D. send the employee home in a tactful manner whenever he reports for duty in an unfit condition

4. In a strike situation, a member of the striking union reports for work but abstains from the full performance of his duties in his normal manner. According to the state civil service law, it is ACCURATE to say that the 4.____
A. employee should be presumed to have engaged in a strike
B. employee should not be presumed to have engaged in a strike
C. city must bear the burden of proving that the employee engaged in a strike
D. city may deny the employee the opportunity to rebut any charge that he engaged in a strike

5. Assume that, as a manager in a health agency which is establishing a *management-by-objective* program, you are asked to review and make recommendations on the following goals set by the agency head for the coming year. 5.____
Which one of these objectives should you recommend dropping because of difficulty in verifying the degree to which the goal has been attained?
A. Establishing night clinics in two preventive health care centers
B. Informing more people of available health services
C. Preparing a training manual for data-processing personnel
D. Producing a 4-page health news bulletin to be distributed monthly to employees

6. The MAIN purpose of the *management-by-objectives* system is to 6.____
A. develop a method of appraising the performance of managerial employees against verifiable objectives rather than against subjective appraisals and personal supervision
B. decentralize managerial decision-making more effectively by setting goals for personnel all the way down to each first-line supervisor as well as to staff people
C. increase managerial accountability and improve managerial effectiveness
D. enable top level managerial employees to impose quantitative goals which will focus attention on the relevant trends that may affect the future

7. Certain city and state employees are on one year's probation for violating the strike provisions of the state civil service law. 7.____
According to a ruling by the state attorney general, in the event of layoffs during their year of probation, the status of these employees should be considered
A. *permanent*, with retention rights based on original date of appointment
B. *probationary*, subject to layoff before permanent employees

C. *permanent*, to be credited with one year less service than indicated by the original date of appointment
D. *probationary*, subject to layoff before other employees in the layoff unit except for those with one year's seniority

8. Assume that, as a senior supervisor conducting a training course for a group of newly assigned first-line supervisors, you emphasize that an effective supervisor should encourage employee suggestions. One member of the group dissents, asserting that many employees come up with worthless, time-wasting ideas. 8.____
The one of the following which would be the MOST appropriate response for you to make is that
A. the supervisor's attitude is wrong, because no suggestion is entirely without merit
B. the supervisor must remember that encouragement of employee suggestions is the major part of any employee development program
C. even if a suggestion seems worthless, the participation of the employee helps to increase his identification with the agency
D. even if a suggestion seems worthless, the supervisor may be able to save it for future use

9. The *grapevine* is an informal channel of communication which exists among employees in an organization as a natural result of their social interaction, and their desire to be kept posted on the latest information. Some information transmitted through the grapevine is truth, some half-truth, and some just rumor. 9.____
Which one of the following would be the MOST appropriate attitude for a member of a management team to have about the grapevine?
A. The grapevine often carries false, malicious, and uncontrollable rumors and management should try to stamp it out by improving official channels of communication.
B. There are more important problems; normally only a small percentage of employees are interested in information transmitted through the grapevine.
C. The grapevine can give management insight into what employees think and feel and can help to supplement the formal communication systems.
D. The grapevine gives employees a harmless outlet for their imagination and an opportunity to relieve their fears and tensions in the form of rumors.

10. Although there are no formal performance appraisal mechanisms for non-managerial employees, managers nevertheless make informal appraisals because some method is needed to measure progress and to let employees know how they are doing. 10.____
The MOST import recent trend in making performance appraisals is toward judging the employee primarily on the extent to which he has
A. tried to perform his assigned tasks
B. demonstrated personal traits which are accepted as necessary to do the job satisfactorily

C. accomplished the objectives set for his job
D. followed the procedures established for the job

11. The proof of a successful human relations program in an organization is the morale crises that never happen. 11.____
Of the following, the implication for managers that follows MOST directly from this statement is that they should
A. review and initiate revisions in all organization policies which may have an adverse effect on employee morale
B. place more emphasis on ability to anticipate and prevent morale problems than on ability to resolve an actual crisis
C. see that first-line supervisors work fairly and understandingly with employees
D. avoid morale crises at all costs, since even the best resolution leaves scar, suspicions, and animosities

12. Suppose that you are conducting a conference on a specific problem. One employee makes a suggestion which you think is highly impractical. 12.____
Of the following, the way for you to respond to this suggestion is FIRST to
A. be frank and tell the employee that his solution is wrong
B. ask the employee in what way his suggestion will solve the problem under discussion
C. refrain from any comment on it, and ask the group whether they have any other solutions to offer
D. ask another participant to point out what is wrong with the suggestion

13. Suppose that a manager notices continuing deterioration in the work, conduct, and interpersonal relationships of one of his immediate subordinates, indicating that this employee has more than a minor emotional problem. Although the manager has made an attempt to help this employee by talking over his problems with him on several occasions, the employee has shown little improvement. 13.____
Of the following, generally the MOST constructive action for the manager to take at this point would be to
A. continue to be supportive by sympathetic listening and counseling
B. show tolerance toward the performance of the disturbed employee
C. discuss the employee's deteriorating condition with him and suggest that he seek professional help
D. consider whether the need of this employee and the agency would be best served by his transfer to another division

14. A manager has a problem involving conflict between two employees concerning a method of performing a work assignment. He does not know the reasons for this conflict. 14.____
The MOST valuable communications method he can use to aid him in resolving the problem is
A. a formal hearing for each employee
B. a staff meeting

C. disciplinary memoranda
D. an informal interview with each employee

15. As a training technique, role-playing is generally considered to be MOST successful when it results in 15.____
A. uncovering the underlying causes of conflict so that any recurrences are prevented
B. recreating an actual work situation which involves conflict among people and in which members of the group simulate specific personalities
C. freeing some people from patterns of rigid thinking and enabling them to look at themselves and others in a new way
D. increasing the participants' powers of logic and reasoning

16. In conducting a disciplinary interview, a supervisor finds that he must ask some highly personal questions which are relevant to the problem at hand. 16.____
The interviewer is MOST likely to get truthful answers to these questions if he asks them
A. early in the interview, before the interviewee has had a chance to become emotional
B. in a manner so that the interviewee can answer them with a simple *yes* or *no*
C. well into the interview, after rapport and trust have been established
D. just after the close of the interview, so that the questions appear to be off the record

17. Suppose that, as a newly assigned manager, you observe that a supervisor in your division uses autocratic methods which are causing resentment among his subordinates. 17.____
Of the following, the MOST likely reason for this supervisor's using such methods is that he
A. was probably exposed to this type of supervision himself
B. does not have an intuitive sense of tact, diplomacy, and consideration and no amount of training can change this
C. received approval for use of such method from his former subordinates
D. does not understand the basic concept of rewards and punishment in the practice of supervision

18. A newly appointed employee, Mr. Jones, was added to the staff of a supervisor who, because of the pressure of other work, turned him over to an experienced subordinate by saying, *Show Mr. Jones around and give him something to do.* 18.____
On the basis of this experience, Mr. Jones' FIRST impression of his new position was most likely to have been
A. *negative*, mainly because it appeared that his job was not worth his supervisor's attention
B. *negative*, mainly because the more experienced subordinate would tend to emphasize the unpleasant aspects of the work
C. *positive*, mainly because his supervisor wasted no time in assigning him to a subordinate
D. *positive*, mainly because he saw himself working for a dynamic supervisor who expected immediate results

19. An employee who stays in one assignment for a number of years often develops a feeling of possessiveness concerning his knowledge of the job which may develop into a problem.
Of the following, the BEST way for a supervisor to remedy this difficulty is to
    A. give the employee less important work to do
    B. point out minor errors as often as possible
    C. raise performance standards for all employees
    D. rotate the employee to a different assignment

19.____

20. A supervisor who tends to be supportive of his subordinates, in contrast to a supervisor who relies upon an authoritarian style of leadership, is more likely, in dealing with his staff, to have to listen to complaints, to have to tolerate emotionally upset employees, and even have to hear unreasonable and insulting remarks.
Compared to the authoritarian supervisor, he is MORE likely to
    A. be unconsciously fearful of failure
    B. have an overriding interest in production
    C. have subordinates who are better educated
    D. receive accurate feedback information

20.____

KEY (CORRECT ANSWERS)

1.	B	11.	B
2.	B	12.	B
3.	B	13.	C
4.	A	14.	D
5.	B	15.	C
6.	C	16.	C
7.	B	17.	A
8.	C	18.	A
9.	C	19.	D
10.	C	20.	D

TEST 2

DIRECTIONS: Each question or incomplete statement is followed by several suggested answers or completions. Select the one that BEST answers the question or completes the statement. *PRINT THE LETTER OF THE CORRECT ANSWER IN THE SPACE AT THE RIGHT.*

1. Assume that one of your subordinates, a supervisor in charge of a small unit in your bureau, asks your advice in handling a situation which has just occurred in his unit. On returning from a meeting, the supervisor notices that Jane Jones, the unit secretary, is not at her regular work location. Another employee had become faint, and the secretary accompanied this employee outdoors for some fresh air. It is a long-standing rule that no employee is permitted to leave the building during office hours except on official business or with the unit head's approval. Quite recently another employee was reprimanded by the supervisor for going out at 10 A.M. for a cup of coffee. 1.____
   Of the following, it would be BEST for you to advise the supervisor to
   A. circulate a memo within the unit, restating the department's regulation concerning leaving the building during office hours
   B. overlook this rule violation in view of the extenuating circumstances
   C. personally reprimand the unit secretary since all employees must be treated in the same way when official rules are broken
   D. tell the unit secretary that you should reprimand her, but that you've decided to overlook the rule infraction this time

2. Of the following, the MOST valid reason why the application of behavioral modification techniques to management of large organizations is not yet widely accepted by managers is these techniques are 2.____
   A. based mainly on research conducted under highly controlled conditions
   B. more readily adaptable to training unskilled employees
   C. incompatible with the validated *management-by-objectives* approach
   D. manipulative and incompatible with the democratic approach

3. Because of intensive pressures which have developed since the onset of the city's financial problems, the members of a certain bureau have begun to file grievances about their working conditions. These protests are accumulating at a much greater rate than normal and faster than they can be disposed of under the current state of affairs. Concerned about the possible effect of these unresolved matters on the productivity of the bureau at such a critical time, the administrator in charge decides to take immediate action to improve staff relations. 3.____
   With this intention in mind, he should
   A. explain to the staff why their grievances cannot be handled at the present time; then inform them that there will be a moratorium on the filing of additional grievances until the current backlog has been eliminated
   B. assemble all grievants at a special meeting and assure them that their problems will be handled in due course, but the current pressures preclude the prompt settling of their grievances

C. assign the assistant directors of the bureau to immediately schedule and conduct hearings on the accumulated grievances until the backlog is eliminated
D. suggest that the grievants again confer with their supervisors about their problems, orally rather than in writing, with direct appeal to him for such cases as are not resolved in this manner

4. A supervisor is attending a staff meeting with other accounting supervisors during which the participants are to propose various possible methods of dealing with a complex operational problem. 4.____
The one of the following procedures which will MOST likely produce an acceptable proposal for solving this problem at this meeting is for the
A. group to agree at the beginning of the meeting on the kinds of approaches to the problem that are most likely to succeed
B. conference leader to set a firm time limit on the period during which the participants are to present whatever ideas come to mind
C. group to discuss each proposal fully before the next proposal is made
D. conference leader to urge every participant in the meeting to present at least one proposal

5. Which one of the following types of communication systems would foster an authoritarian atmosphere in a large agency? 5.____
A communication system which
A. is restricted to organizational procedures and specific job instructions
B. provides information to employees about the rationale for their jobs
C. informs employees about their job performance
D. provides information about the relationship of employees' work to the agency's goals

6. According to most management experts, the one of the following which would generally have SERIOUS shortcomings as a component of a performance evaluation program is 6.____
A. rating the performance of each subordinate against the performance of other subordinates
B. limiting the appraisal to an evaluation of current performance
C. rating each subordinate in terms of clearly stated, measurable job goals
D. interviewing the subordinate to discuss present job performance and ways of improvement

7. Which of the following is consistent with the management-by-objectives approach as used in a fiscal affairs division of a large city agency? 7.____
A. Performance goals for the division are established by the administrator, who requires daily progress reports for each accounting unit.
B. Each subordinate accountant participates in setting his own short-term performance goals.
C. A detailed set of short-term performance goals for each accountant is prepared by his supervisor.
D. Objectives are established and progress evaluated by a committee of administrative accountants.

Questions 8-11.

DIRECTIONS: Questions 8 through 11 are to be answered on the basis of the following information.

Assume that you are the director of a small bureau, organized into three divisions. The bureau has a total of twenty employees: fourteen in professional titles and six in clerical titles. Each division has a chief who reports directly to you and who supervises five employees.

For Questions 8 through 11, you are to select the MOST appropriate training method, from the four choices given, based on the situation in the question:

A. Lecture, with a small blackboard available
B. Lecture, with audio-visual aids
C. Conference
D. Buddy system (experienced worker is accompanied by worker to be trained)

8. A major reorganization of your department was completed. You have decided to conduct a training session of about one hour's duration for all your subordinates in order to acquaint them with the new departmental structure as well as the new responsibilities which have been assigned to the divisions of your bureau. 8.____

9. Three assistant supervisors, each with one year of service in your department, are transferred to your bureau as part of the process of strengthening the major activity of your bureau. In connection with their duties, if they are required to do field visits to business firms located in the various industrial areas of the city. 9.____

10. The work of your bureau requires that various forms be processed sequentially through each of three divisions. In recent weeks, you have received complaints from the division chiefs that their production is being impeded by a lack of cooperation from the chiefs and workers in the other divisions. 10.____

11. In order to improve the efficiency of the department, your department head has directed that all bureaus hold weekly, thirty-minute-long training sessions for all employees, to review relevant work procedures. 11.____

12. Which one of the following actions is usually MOST appropriate for a manager to take in order to encourage and develop coordination of effort among different units or individuals within an organization? 12.____
    A. Providing rewards to the most productive employees
    B. Giving employees greater responsibility and the authority to exercise it
    C. Emphasizing to the employees that it is important to coordinate their efforts
    D. Explaining the goals of the organization to the employees and how their jobs relate to those goals

13. The management of time is one of the critical aspects of any supervisor's performance. 13.____
Therefore, in evaluating a subordinate from the viewpoint of how he manages time, a supervisor should rate HIGHEST the subordinate who
   A. concentrates on each task as he undertakes it
   B. performs at a standard and predictable pace under all circumstances
   C. takes shortened lunch periods when he is busy
   D. tries to do two things simultaneously

14. A MAJOR research finding regarding employee absenteeism is that 14.____
   A. absenteeism is likely to be higher on hot days
   B male employees tend to be absent more than female employees
   C. the way an employee is treated as a definite bearing on absenteeism
   D. the distance employees have to travel is one of the most important factors in absenteeism

15. Of the following, the supervisory behavior that is of GREATEST benefit to the organization is exhibited by supervisors who 15.____
   A. are strict with subordinates about following rules and regulations
   B. encourage subordinates to be interested in the work
   C. are willing to assist with subordinates' work on most occasions
   D. get the most done with available staff and resources

16. In order to maintain a proper relationship with a worker who is assigned to staff rather than line functions, a line supervisor should 16.____
   A. accept all recommendations of the staff worker
   B. include the staff worker in the conferences called by the supervisor for his subordinates
   C. keep the staff worker informed of developments in the area of his staff assignment
   D. require that the staff worker's recommendations be communicated to the supervisor through the supervisor's own superior

17. Of the following, the GREATEST disadvantage of placing a worker in a staff position under the direct supervision of the supervisor whom he advises is the possibility that the 17.____
   A. staff worker will tend to be insubordinate because of a feeling of superiority over the supervisor
   B. staff worker will tend to give advice of the type which the supervisor wants to hear or finds acceptable
   C. supervisor will tend to be mistrustful of the advice of a worker of subordinate rank
   D. supervisor will tend to derive little benefit from the advice because to supervise properly he should know at least as much as his subordinate

18. One factor which might be given consideration in deciding upon the optimum span of control of a supervisor over his immediate subordinates is the position of the supervisor in the hierarchy of the organization. 18.____
It is generally considered proper that the number of subordinates immediately supervised by a higher, upper echelon, supervisor
   A. is unrelated to and tends to form no pattern with the number of supervised by lower level supervisors
   B. should be about the same as the number supervised by a lower level supervisor
   C. should be larger than the number supervised by a lower level supervisor
   D. should be smaller than the number supervised by a lower level supervisor

19. Assume that you are a supervisor and have been assigned to assist the head of a large agency unit. He asks you to prepare a simple, functional organization chart of the unit. 19.____
Such a chart would be USEFUL for
   A. favorably impressing members of the public with the important nature of the agency's work
   B. graphically presenting staff relationships which may indicate previously unknown duplications, overlaps, and gaps in job duties
   C. motivating all employees toward better performance because they will have a better understanding of job procedures
   D. subtly and inoffensively making known to the staff in the unit that you are now in a position of responsibility

20. In some large organizations, management's traditional means of learning about employee dissatisfaction has been in the *open door policy*. 20.____
This policy USUALLY means that
   A. management lets it be known that a management representative is generally available to discuss employees' questions, suggestions, and complaints
   B. management sets up an informal employee organization to establish a democratic procedure for orderly representation of employees
   C. employees are encouraged to attempt to resolve dissatisfactions at the lowest possible level of authority
   D. employees are provided with an address or box so that they may safely and anonymously register complaints

KEY (CORRECT ANSWERS)

1.	B	11.	A
2.	A	12.	D
3.	D	13.	A
4.	B	14.	C
5.	A	15.	D
6.	A	16.	C
7.	B	17.	B
8.	B	18.	D
9.	D	19.	B
10.	C	20.	A

EXAMINATION SECTION

TEST 1

DIRECTIONS: Each question or incomplete statement is followed by several suggested answers or completions. Select the one that BEST answers the question or completes the statement. *PRINT THE LETTER OF THE CORRECT ANSWER IN THE SPACE AT THE RIGHT.*

Questions 1-5.

DIRECTIONS: Each of Questions 1 through 5 consists of a passage which contains one word that is incorrectly used because it is not in keeping with the meaning that the quotation is evidently intended to convey. Determine which word is incorrectly used. Select from the choices lettered A, B, C, and D the word which, when substituted for the incorrectly used word, would BEST to convey the meaning of the quotation.

1. Whatever the method, the necessity to keep up with the dynamics of an organization is the point on which many classification plans go awry. The budgetary approach to "positions," for example, often leads to using for recruitment and pay purposes a position authorized many years earlier for quite a different purpose than currently contemplated—making perhaps the title, the class, and the qualifications required inappropriate to the current need. This happens because executives overlook the stability that takes place in job duties and fail to reread an initial description of the job before saying, as they scan a list of titles, "We should fill this position right away." Once a classification plan is adopted, it is pointless to do anything less than provide for continuous, painstaking maintenance on a current basis, else once different positions that have actually become similar to each other remain in different classes, and some former cognates that have become quite different continue in the same class. Such a program often seems expensive. But to stint too much on this out-of-pocket cost may create still higher hidden costs growing out of lowered morale, poor production, delayed operating programs, excessive pay for simple work, and low pay for responsible work (resulting in poorly qualified executives and professional men)—all normal concomitants of inadequate, hasty, or out-of-date classification. 1.____

   A. evolution B. personnel C. disapproved D. forward

2. At first sight, it may seem that there is little or no difference between the usableness of a manual and the degree of its use. But there is a difference. A manual may have all the qualities which make up the usable manual and still not be used. Take this instance as an example: Suppose you have a satisfactory manual but issue instructions from day to day through the avenue of bulletins, memorandums, and other informational releases. Which will the employee use, the manual or the bulletin which passes over his desk? He will, 2.____

of course, use the latter, for some obsolete material will not be contained in this manual. Here we have a theoretically usable manual which is unused because of the other avenues by which procedural information may be issued.

A. countermand B. discard C. intentional D. worthwhile

3. By reconcentrating control over its operations in a central headquarters, a firm is able to extend the influence of automation to many, if not all, of its functions—from inventory and payroll to production, sales, and personnel. In so doing, businesses freeze all the elements of the corporate function in their relationship to one another and to the overall objectives of the firm. From this total systems concept, companies learn that computers can accomplish much more than clerical and accounting jobs. Their capabilities can be tapped to perform the traditional applications (payroll processing, inventory control, accounts payable, and accounts receivable) as well as newer applications such as spotting deviations from planned programs (exception reporting), adjusting planning schedules, forecasting business trends, simulating market conditions, and solving production problems. Since the officer manage is a manager of information and each of these applications revolve around the processing of data, he must take an active role in studying and improving the system under his care. 3.____

A. maintaining B. inclusion C. limited D. visualize

4. In addition to the formal and acceptance theories of the source of authority, although perhaps more closely related to the latter, is the belief that authority is generated by personal qualifies of technical competence. Under this heading is the individual who has made, in effect, subordinates of others through sheer force of personality, and the engineer or economist who exerts influence by furnishing answers or sound advice. These may have no actual organizational authority, yet their advice may be so eagerly sought and so unerringly followed that it appears to carry the weight of an order. But, above all, one cannot discount the importance of formal authority with its institutional foundations. Buttressed by the qualities of leadership implicit in the acceptance theory, formal authority is basic to the managerial job. Once abrogated, it may be delegated or withheld, used or misused, and be effective in capable hands or be ineffective in inept hands. 4.____

A. selected B. delegation C. limited D. possessed

5. Since managerial operations in organization, staffing, directing, and controlling are designed to support the accomplishment of enterprise objectives, planning logically precedes the execution of all other managerial functions. Although all the functions intermesh in practice, planning is unique in that it establishes the objectives necessary for all group effort. Besides, plans must be made to accomplish these objectives before the manager knows what kind of organization relationships and personal qualifications are needed, along which course subordinates are to be directed, and what kind of control is to be applied. And, of course, each of the other managerial functions must be planned if they are to be effective. 5.____

Planning and control are inseparable—the Siamese twins of management. Unplanned action cannot be controlled, for control involves keeping activities on course by correcting deviations from plans. Any attempt to control without plans would be meaningless, since there are no way anyone can tell whether he is going where he wants to go—the task of control—unless first he knows where he wants to go—the task of planning. Plans thus preclude the standards of control.

A. coordinating B. individual C. furnish D. follow

Questions 6-7.

DIRECTIONS: Questions 6 and 7 are to be answered SOLELY on the basis of information given in the following paragraph.

In-basket tests are often used to assess managerial potential. The exercise consists of a set of papers that would be likely to be found in the in-basket of an administrator or manager at any given time, and requires the individuals participating in the examination to indicate how they would dispose of each item found in the in-basket. In order to handle the in-basket effectively, they must successfully manage their time, refer and assign some work to subordinates, juggle potentially conflicting appointments and meetings, and arrange for follow-up of problems generated by the items in the in-basket. In other words, the in-basket test is attempting to evaluate the participants' abilities to organize their work, set priorities, delegate control, and make decisions.

6. According to the above paragraph, to succeed in an in-basket test, an administrator must 6.____
   A. be able to read very quickly
   B. have a great deal of technical knowledge
   C. know when to delegate work
   D. arrange a lot of appointments and meetings

7. According to the above paragraph, all of the following abilities are indications of managerial potential EXCEPT the ability to 7.____
   A. organize and control
   B. manage time
   C. write effective reports
   D. make appropriate decisions

Questions 8-9.

DIRECTIONS: Questions 8 and 9 are to be answered SOLELY on the basis of information given in the following paragraph.

One of the biggest mistakes of government executives with substantial supervisory responsibility is failing to make careful appraisals of performance during employee probationary periods. Many a later headache could have been avoided by prompt and full appraisal during the early months of an employee's assignment. There is not much more to say about this except to emphasize the common prevalence of this oversight, and to underscore that for its consequences, which are many and sad, the offending managers have no one to blame but themselves.

8. According to the above paragraph, probationary periods are 8.____
   A. a mistake, and should not be used by supervisors with large responsibilities
   B. not used properly by government executives
   C. used only for those with supervisory responsibility
   D. the consequences of management mistakes

9. The one of the following conclusions that can MOST appropriately be drawn from the above paragraph is that 9.____
   A. management's failure to appraise employees during their probationary period is a common occurrence
   B. there is not much to say about probationary periods, because they are unimportant
   C. managers should blame employees for failing to use their probationary periods properly
   D. probationary periods are a headache to most managers

Questions 10-12.

DIRECTIONS: Questions 11 and 12 are to be answered SOLELY on the basis of the information given in the following paragraph.

The common sense character of the merit system seems so natural to most Americans that many people wonder why it should ever have been inoperative. After all, the American economic system, the most phenomenal the world has ever known, is also founded on a rugged selective process which emphasizes the personal qualities of capacity, industriousness, and productivity. The criteria may not have always been appropriate and competition has not always been fair, but competition there was, and the responsibilities and the rewards—with exceptions, of course—have gone to those who could measure up in terms of intelligence, knowledge, or perseverance. This has been true not only in the economic area, in the money-making process, but also in achievement in the professions and other walks of life.

10. According to the above paragraph, economic awards in the United States have 10.____
    A. always been based on appropriate, fair criteria
    B. only recently been based on a competitive system
    C. not gone to people who compete too ruggedly
    D. usually gone to those people with intelligence, knowledge, and perseverance

11. According to the above paragraph, a merit system is 11.____
    A. an unfair criterion on which to base rewards
    B. unnatural to anyone who is not American
    C. based only on common sense
    D. based on the same principles as the American economic system

12. According to the above paragraph, it is MOST accurate to say that 12.____
    A. the United States has always had a civil service merit system
    B. civil service employees are very rugged
    C. the American economic system has always been based on a merit objective
    D. competition is unique to the American way of life

Questions 13-15.

DIRECTIONS: The management study of employee absence due to sickness is an effective tool in planning. Questions 13 through 15 are to be answered SOLELY on the data given below.

Number of Days Absent Per Worker (Sickness)	1	2	3	4	5	6	7	8 or Over
Number of Workers	76	23	6	3	1	0	1	0
Total Number of Workers	400							
Period Covered	January 1 – December 31							

13. The total number of man-days lost due to illness was 13.____
    A. 110 B. 137 C. 144 D. 164

14. What percent of the workers had 4 or more days absence due to sickness? 14.____
    A. .25% B. 2.5% C. 1.25% D. 12.5%

15. Of the 400 workers studied, the number who lost no days due to sickness was 15.____
    A. 190 B. 236 C. 290 D. 346

Questions 16-18.

DIRECTIONS: In the graph below, the lines labeled "A" and "B" represent the cumulative progress in the work of two file clerks, each of whom was given 500 consecutively numbered applications to file in the proper cabinets over a five-day work week. Questions 16 through 18 are to be answered SOLELY upon the data provided in the graph.

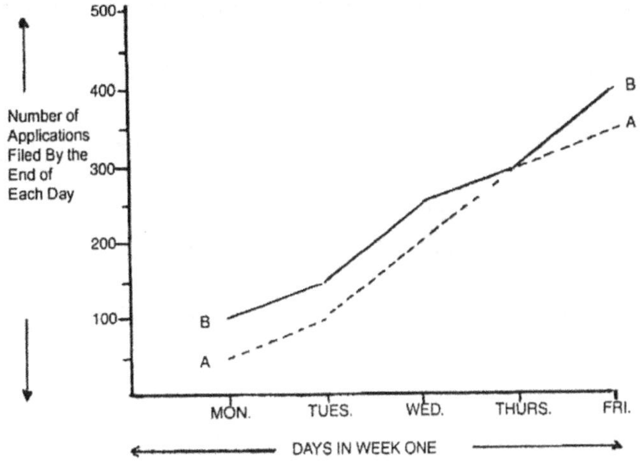

16. The day during which the LARGEST number of applications was filed by both clerks was 16.____
    A. Monday B. Tuesday C. Wednesday D. Friday

17. At the end of the second day, the percentage of applications STILL to be filed was 17.____
    A. 25% B. 50% C. 66% D. 75%

18. Assuming that the production pattern is the same the following week as the week shown in the chart, the day on which the file clerks will FINISH this assignment will be 18.____
    A. Monday B. Tuesday C. Wednesday D. Friday

Questions 19-21.

DIRECTIONS: The following chart shows the differences between the rates of production of employees in Department D in 2009 and 2019. Questions 19 through 21 are to be answered SOLELY on the basis of the information given in the chart.

Number of Employees Producing Work-Units Within Range in 2009	Number of Work-Units Produced	Number of Employees Producing Work-Units Within Range in 2019
7	500 – 1000	4
14	1001 – 1500	11
26	1501 – 2000	28
22	2001 – 2500	36
17	2501 – 3000	39
10	3001 – 3500	23
4	3501 - 4000	9

19. Assuming that within each range of work-units produced the average production was at the mid-point at that range (e.g., category 500 – 1000 = 750), then the AVERAGE number of work-units produced per employee in 2009 fell into the range 19.____
    A. 1001 – 1500 B. 1501 – 2000 C. 2001 – 2500 D. 2501 – 3000

20. The ratio of the number of employees producing more than 2000 work-units in 2009 to the number of employees producing more than 2000 work-units in 2019 is MOST NEARLY 20.____
    A. 1:2 B. 2:3 C. 3:4 D. 4:5

21. In Department D, which of the following were GREATER in 2019 than in 2009? 21.____
    I. Total number of employees
    II. Total number of work-units produced
    III. Number of employees producing 2000 or fewer work-units
    The CORRECT answer is
    A. I, II, III B. I, II C. I, III D. II, III

22. Unit S's production fluctuated substantially from one year to another. In 2018, Unit S's production was 100% greater than in 2017. In 2019, production decreased by 25% from 2018. In 2020, Unit S's production was 10% greater than in 2019. 22.____
On the basis of this information, it is CORRECT to conclude that Unit S's production in 2020 exceeded Unit S's production in 2017 by
A. 65% B. 85% C. 95% D. 135%

23. Agency "X" is moving into a new building. It has 1500 employees presently on its staff and does not contemplate much variance from this level. The new building contains 100 available offices, each with a maximum capacity of 30 employees. It has been decided that only 2/3 of the maximum capacity of each office will be utilized. 23.____
The TOTAL number of offices that will be occupied by Agency "X" is
A. 30 B. 66 C. 75 D. 90

24. One typist completes a form letter every 5 minutes and another typist completes one every 6 minutes. 24.____
If the two typists start together, they will again start typing new letters simultaneously _____ minutes later and will have completed _____ letters by that time.
A. 11; 30 B. 12; 24 C. 24; 12 D. 30; 11

25. During one week, a machine operator produces 10 fewer pages per hour of work than he usually does. 25.____
If it ordinarily takes him six hours to produce a 300-page report, it will take him _____ hours longer to produce that same 300-page report during the week when he produces more slowly.
A. 1½ B. $1^2/_3$ C. 2 D. 2¾

KEY (CORRECT ANSWERS)

		Incorrect Words
1.	A	stability
2.	D	obsolete
3.	D	freeze
4.	D	abrogated
5.	C	preclude

6.	C	16.	C
7.	C	17.	D
8.	B	18.	B
9.	A	19.	C
10.	D	20.	A
11.	D	21.	B
12	C	22.	A
13.	D	23.	C
14.	C	24.	D
15.	C	25.	A

REPORT WRITING

EXAMINATION SECTION

TEST 1

DIRECTIONS: Each question or incomplete statement is followed by several suggested answers or completions. Select the one that BEST answers the question or completes the statement. *PRINT THE LETTER OF THE CORRECT ANSWER IN THE SPACE AT THE RIGHT.*

Questions 1-4.

DIRECTIONS: Answer Questions 1 through 4 on the basis of the following report which was prepared by a supervisor for inclusion in his agency's annual report.

On Oct. 13, I was assigned to study the salaries paid. to clerical employees in various titles by the city and by private industry in the area.

In order to get the data I needed, I called Mr. Johnson at the Bureau of the Budget and the payroll officers at X Corp.— a brokerage house, Y Co. —an insurance company, and Z Inc. — a publishing firm. None of them was available and I had to call all of them again the next day.

When I finally got the information I needed, I drew up a chart, which is attached. Note that not all of the companies I contacted employed people at all the different levels used in the city service.

The conclusions I draw from analyzing this information is as follows: The city's entry-level salary is about average for the region; middle-level salaries are generally higher in the city government plan than in private industry; but salaries at the highest levels in private industry are better than city employees' pay.

1. Which of the following criticisms about the style in which this report is written is MOST valid? 1.____
   A. It is too informal.
   B. It is too concise.
   C. It is too choppy.
   D. The syntax is too complex.

2. Judging from the statements made in the report, the method followed by this employee in performing his research was 2.____
   A. *good*; he contacted a representative sample of businesses in the area
   B. *poor*; he should have drawn more definite conclusions
   C. *good*; he was persistent in collecting information
   D. *poor*; he did not make a thorough study

3. One sentence in this report contains a grammatical error. This sentence begins on line number 3.____
   A. 4 B. 7 C. 10 D. 14

4. The type of information given in this report which should be presented in footnotes or in an appendix is the 4.____
   A. purpose of the study
   B. specifics about the businesses contacted
   C. reference to the chart
   D. conclusions drawn by the author

5. The use of a graph to show statistical data in a report is SUPERIOR to a table because it 5.____
   A. features approximations
   B. emphasizes facts and relationships more dramatically
   C. presents data more accurately
   D. is easily understood by the average reader

6. Of the following, the degree of formality required of a written report in tone is MOST likely to depend on the 6.____
   A. subject matter of the report
   B. frequency of its occurrence
   C. amount of time available for its preparation
   D. audience for whom the report is intended

7. Of the following, a distinguishing characteristic of a written report intended for the head of your agency as compared to a report prepared for a lower-echelon staff member is that the report for the agency head should USUALLY include 7.____
   A. considerably more detail, especially statistical data
   B. the essential details in an abbreviated form
   C. all available source material
   D. an annotated bibliography

8. Assume that you are asked to write a lengthy report for use by the administrator of your agency, the subject of which is "The Impact of Proposed New Data Processing Operation on Line Personnel" in your agency. You decide that the *most* appropriate type of report for you to prepare is an analytical report, including recommendations. 8.____
   The MAIN reason for your decision is that
   A. the subject of the report is extremely complex
   B. large sums of money are involved
   C. the report is being prepared for the administrator
   D. you intend to include charts and graphs

9. Assume that you are preparing a report based on a survey dealing with the attitudes of employees in Division X regarding proposed new changes in compensating employees for working overtime. Three percent of the respondents to the survey voluntarily offer an unfavorable opinion on the method of assigning overtime work, a question not specifically asked of the employees. 9.____
On the basis of this information, the MOST appropriate and significant of the following comments for you to make in the report with regard to employees' attitudes on assigning overtime work is that
   A. an insignificant percentage of employees dislike the method of assigning overtime work
   B. three percent of the employees in Division X dislike the method of assigning overtime work
   C. three percent of the sample selected for the survey voiced an unfavorable opinion on the method of assigning overtime work
   D. some employees voluntarily voiced negative feelings about the method of assigning overtime work, making it impossible to determine the extent of this attitude

10. A supervisor should be able to prepare a report that is well-written and unambiguous. 10.____
Of the following sentences that might appear in a report, select the one which communicates MOST clearly the intent of its author.
   A. When your subordinates speak to a group of people, they should be well-informed.
   B. When he asked him to leave, SanMan King told him that he would refuse the request.
   C. Because he is a good worker, Foreman Jefferson assigned Assistant Foreman D'Agostino to replace him.
   D. Each of us is responsible for the actions of our subordinates.

11. In some reports, especially longer ones, a list of the resources (books, papers, magazines, etc.) used to prepare it is included. This list is called the 11.____
   A. accreditation
   B. bibliography
   C. summary
   D. glossary

12. Reports are usually divided into several sections, some of which are more necessary than others. 12.____
Of the following, the section which is ABSOLUTELY necessary to include in a report is
   A. a table of contents
   B. the body
   C. an index
   D. a bibliography

13. Suppose you are writing a report on an interview you have just completed with a particularly hostile applicant. 13.____
Which of the following BEST describes what you should include in this report?
A. What you think caused the applicant's hostile attitude during the interview
B. Specific examples of the applicant's hostile remarks and behavior
C. The relevant information uncovered during the interview
D. A recommendation that the applicant's request be denied because of his hostility

14. When including recommendations in a report to your supervisor, which of the following is MOST important for you to do? 14.____
A. Provide several alternative courses of action for each recommendation
B. First present the supporting evidence, then the recommendations
C. First present the recommendations, then the supporting evidence
D. Make sure the recommendations arise logically out of the information in the report

15. It is often necessary that the writer of a report present facts and sufficient arguments to gain acceptance of the points, conclusions, or recommendations set forth in the report. 15.____
Of the following, the LEAST advisable step to take in organizing a report, when such argumentation is the important factor, is a(n)
A. elaborate expression of personal belief
B. businesslike discussion of the problem as a whole
C. orderly arrangement of convincing data
D. reasonable explanation of the primary issues

16. In some types of reports, visual aids add interest, meaning, and support. They also provide an essential means of effectively communicating the message of the report. 16.____
Of the following, the selection of the suitable visual aids to use with a report is LEAST dependent on the
A. nature and scope of the report
B. way in which the aid is to be used
C. aid used in other reports
D. prospective readers of the report

17. Visual aids used in a report may be placed either in the text material or in the appendix. 17.____
Deciding where to put a chart, table, or any such aid should depend on the
A. title of the report
B. purpose of the visual aid
C. title of the visual aid
D. length of the report

18. A report is often revised several times before final preparation and distribution in an effort to make certain the report meets the needs of the situation for which it is designed. 18.____
Which of the following is the BEST way for the author to be sure that a report covers the areas he intended?

A. Obtain a coworker's opinion
B. Compare it with a content checklist
C. Test it on a subordinate
D. Check his bibliography

19. In which of the following situations is an oral report preferable to a written report? When a(n) 19.____
A. recommendation is being made for a future plan of action
B. department head requests immediate information
C. long-standing policy change is made
D. analysis of complicated statistical data is involved

20. When an applicant is approved, the supervisor must fill in standard forms with certain information. 20.____
The GREATEST advantage of using standard forms in this situation rather than having the supervisor write the report as he sees fit is that
A. the report can be acted on quickly
B. the report can be written without directions from a supervisor
C. needed information is less likely to be left out of the report
D. information that is written up this way is more likely to be verified

21. Assume that it is part of your job to prepare a monthly report for your unit head that eventually goes to the director. The report contains information on the number of applicants you have interviewed that have been approved and the number of applicants you have interviewed that have been turned down. 21.____
Errors on such reports are serious because
A. you are expected to be able to prove how many applicants you have interviewed each month
B. accurate statistics are needed for effective management of the department
C. they may not be discovered before the report is transmitted to the director
D. they may result in loss to the applicants left out of the report

22. The frequency with which job reports are submitted should depend MAINLY on 22.____
A. how comprehensive the report has to be
B. the amount of information in the report
C. the availability of an experienced man to write the report
D. the importance of changes in the information included in the report

23. The CHIEF purpose in preparing an outline for a report is usually to insure that 23.____
A. the report will be grammatically correct
B. every point will be given equal emphasis
C. principal and secondary points will be properly integrated
D. the language of the report will be of the same level and include the same technical terms

24. The MAIN reason for requiring written job reports is to 24.____
    A. avoid the necessity of oral orders
    B. develop better methods of doing the work
    C. provide a permanent record of what was done
    D. increase the amount of work that can be done

25. Assume you are recommending in a report to your supervisor that a radical change in a standard maintenance procedure should be adopted. 25.____
Of the following, the MOST important information to be included in this report is
    A. a list of the reasons for making this change
    B. the names of others who favor the change
    C. a complete description of the present procedure
    D. amount of training time needed for the new procedure

KEY (CORRECT ANSWERS)

1.	A	11.	B
2.	D	12.	B
3.	D	13.	C
4.	B	14.	D
5.	B	15.	A
6.	D	16.	C
7.	B	17.	B
8.	A	18.	B
9.	D	19.	B
10.	D	20.	C

21.	B
22.	D
23.	C
24.	C
25.	A

TEST 2

DIRECTIONS: Each question or incomplete statement is followed by several suggested answers or completions. Select the one that BEST answers the question or completes the statement. *PRINT THE LETTER OF THE CORRECT ANSWER IN THE SPACE AT THE RIGHT.*

1. It is often necessary that the writer of a report present facts and sufficient arguments to gain acceptance of the points, conclusions, or recommendations set forth in the report. 1.____
Of the following, the LEAST advisable step to take in organizing a report, when such argumentation is the important factor, is a(n)
   A. elaborate expression of personal belief
   B. businesslike discussion of the problem as a whole
   C. orderly arrangement of convincing data
   D. reasonable explanation of the primary issues

2. Of the following, the factor which is generally considered to be LEAST characteristic of a good control report is that it 2.____
   A. stresses performance that adheres to standard rather than emphasizing the exception
   B. supplies information intended to serve as the basis for corrective action
   C. provides feedback for the planning process
   D. includes data that reflect trends as well as current status

3. An administrative assistant has been asked by his superior to write a concise, factual report with objective conclusions and recommendations based on facts assembled by other researchers. 3.____
Of the following factors, the administrative assistant should give LEAST consideration to
   A. the educational level of the person or persons for whom the report is being prepared
   B. the use to be made of the report
   C. the complexity of the problem
   D. his own feelings about the importance of the problem

4. When making a written report, it is often recommended that the findings or conclusions be presented near the beginning of the report. 4.____
Of the following, the MOST important reason for doing this is that it
   A. facilitates organizing the material clearly
   B. assures that all the topics will be covered
   C. avoids unnecessary repetition of ideas
   D. prepares the reader for the facts that will follow

5. You have been asked to write a report on methods of hiring and training new employees. Your report is going to be about ten pages long. 5.____
For the convenience of your readers, a brief summary of your findings should
   A. appear at the beginning of your report
   B. be appended to the report as a postscript
   C. be circulated in a separate memo
   D. be inserted in tabular form in the middle of your report

6. In preparing a report, the MAIN reason for writing an outline is usually to 6.____
   A. help organize thoughts in a logical sequence
   B. provide a guide for the typing of the report
   C. allow the ultimate user to review the report in advance
   D. ensure that the report is being prepared on schedule

7. The one of the following which is MOST appropriate as a reason for including footnotes in a report is to 7.____
   A. correct capitalization
   B. delete passages
   C. improve punctuation
   D. cite references

8. A completed formal report may contain all of the following EXCEPT 8.____
   A. a synopsis
   B. a preface
   C. marginal notes
   D. bibliographical references

9. Of the following, the MAIN use of proofreaders' marks is to 9.____
   A. explain corrections to be made
   B. indicate that a manuscript has been read and approved
   C. let the reader know who proofread the report
   D. indicate the format of the report

10. Informative, readable, and concise reports have been found to observe the following rules: 10.____
   Rule I. Keep the report short and easy to understand
   Rule II. Vary the length of sentences.
   Rule III. Vary the style of sentences so that, for example, they are not all just subject-verb, subject-verb.

Consider this hospital laboratory report: The experiment was started in January. The apparatus was put together in six weeks. At that time, the synthesizing process was begun. The synthetic chemicals were separated. Then they were used in tests on patients.
Which one of the following choices MOST accurately classifies the above rules into those which are violated by this report ad those which are not?
   A. II is violated, but I and III are not.
   B. III is violated, but I and II are not.
   C. II and III are violated, but I is not.
   D. I, II, and III are violated,

Questions 11-13.

DIRECTIONS: Questions 11 through 13 are based on the following example of a report. The report consists of eight numbered sentences, some of which are not consistent with the principles of good report writing.

(1) I interviewed Mrs. Loretta Crawford in Room 424 of County Hospital. (2) She had collapsed on the street and been brought into emergency. (3) She is an attractive woman with many friends judging by the cards she had received. (4) She did not know what her husband's last job had been, or what their present income was. (5) The first thing that Mrs. Crawford said was that she had never worked and that her husband was presently unemployed. (6) She did not know if they had any medical coverage or if they could pay the bill. (7) She said that her husband could not be reached by telephone but that he would be in to see her that afternoon. (8) I left word at the nursing station to be called when he arrived.

11. A good report should be arranged in logical order. 11.____
Which of the following sentences from the report does NOT appear in its proper sequence in the report?
A. 1 B. 4 C. 7 D. 8

12. Only material that is relevant to the main thought of a report should be included. 12.____
Which of the following sentences from the report contains material which is LEAST relevant to this report? Sentence
A. 3 B. 4 C. 6 D. 8

13. Reports should include all essential information. 13.____
Of the following, the MOST important fact that is missing from this report is:
A. Who was involved in the interview
B. What was discovered at the interview
C. When the interview took place
D. Where the interview took place

Questions 14-15.

DIRECTIONS: Each of Questions 14 and 15 consists of four numbered sentences which constitute a paragraph in a report. They are not in the right order. Choose the numbered arrangement appearing after letter A, B, C, or D which is MOST logical and which BEST expresses the thought of the paragraph.

14. I. Congress made the commitment explicit in the Housing Act of 1949, establishing as a national goal the realization of a decent home and suitable environment for every American family. 14.____
II. The result has been that the goal of decent home and suitable environment is still as far distant as ever for the disadvantaged urban family
III. In spite of this action by Congress, federal housing programs have continued to be fragmented and grossly under-funded.
IV. The passage of the National Housing Act signaled a new federal commitment to provide housing for the nation's citizens.

The CORRECT answer is:
A. I, IV, III, II B. IV, I, III, II C. IV, I, III, II D. II, IV, I, III

15. I. The greater expense does not necessarily involve "exploitation," but it is often perceived as exploitative and unfair by those who are aware of the price differences involved, but unaware of operating costs. 15.____
II. Ghetto residents believe they are "exploited" by local merchants, and evidence substantiates some of these beliefs.
III. However, stores in low-income areas were more likely to be small independents, which could not achieve the economies available to supermarket chains and were, therefore, more likely to charge higher prices, and the customers were more likely to buy smaller-sized packages which are more expensive per unit of measure.
IV. A study conducted in one city showed that distinctly higher prices were charged for goods sold in ghetto stores than in other areas.

The CORRECT answer is:
A. IV, II, I, III B. IV, I, III, II C. II, IV, III, I D. II, III, IV, I

16. In organizing data to be presented in a formal report, the FIRST of the following steps should be 16.____
A. determining the conclusions to be drawn
B. establishing the time sequence of the data
C. sorting and arranging like data into groups
D. evaluating how consistently the data support the recommendations

17. All reports should be prepared with at least one copy so that 17.____
A. there is one copy for your file
B. there is a copy for your supervisor
C. the report can be sent to more than one person
D. the person getting the report can forward a copy to someone else

18. Before turning in a report of an investigation he has made, a supervisor discovers some additional information he did not include in this report. Whether he rewrites this report to include this additional information should PRIMARILY depend on the 18.____
A. importance of the report itself
B. number of people who will eventually review this report
C. established policy covering the subject matter of the report
D. bearing this new information has on the conclusions of the report

KEY (CORRECT ANSWERS)

1.	A	11.	B
2.	A	12.	A
3.	D	13.	C
4.	D	14.	B
5.	A	15.	C
6.	A	16.	C
7.	D	17.	A
8.	C	18.	D
9.	A		
10.	C		

PRINCIPLES AND PRACTICES, OF ADMINISTRATION, SUPERVISION AND MANAGEMENT

TABLE OF CONTENTS

PRINCIPLES AND PRACTICES, OF ADMINISTRATION, SUPERVISION AND MANAGEMENT

Most people are inclined to think of administration as something that only a few persons are responsible for in a large organization. Perhaps this is true if you are thinking of Administration with a capital *A*, but administration with a lower case *a* is a responsibility of supervisors at all levels each working day.

All of us feel we are pretty good supervisors and that we do a good job of administering the workings of our agency. By and large, this is true, but every so often it is good to check up on ourselves. Checklists appear from time to time in various publications which psychologists say tell whether or not a person will make a good wife, husband, doctor, lawyer, or supervisor.

The following questions are an excellent checklist to test yourself as a supervisor and administrator.

Remember, Administration gives direction and points the way but administration carries the ideas to fruition. Each is dependent on the other for its success. Remember, too, that no unit is too small for these departmental functions to be carried out. These statements apply equally as well to the Chief Librarian as to the Department Head with but one or two persons to supervise.

GENERAL ADMINISTRATION: General Responsibilities of Supervisors

1. Have I prepared written statements of functions, activities, and duties for my organizational unit?

2. Have I prepared procedural guides for operating activities?

3. Have I established clearly in writing, lines of authority and responsibility for my organizational unit?

4. Do I make recommendations for improvements in organization, policies, administrative and operating routines and procedures, including simplification of work and elimination of non-essential operations?

5. Have I designated and trained an understudy to function in my absence?

6. Do I supervise and train personnel within the unit to effectively perform their assignments?

7. Do I assign personnel and distribute work on such a basis as to carry out the organizational unit's assignment or mission in the most effective and efficient manner?

8. Have I established administrative controls by:

    a. Fixing responsibility and accountability on all supervisors under my direction for the proper performance of their functions and duties.

b. Preparations and submitting periodic work load and progress reports covering the operations of the unit to my immediate superior.

c. Analysis and evaluation of such reports received from subordinate units.

d. Submission of significant developments and problems arising within the organizational unit to my immediate superior.

e. Conducting conferences, inspections, etc., as to the status and efficiency of unit operations.

9. Do I maintain an adequate and competent working force?

10. Have I fostered good employee-department relations, seeing that established rules, regulations, and instructions are being carried out properly?

11. Do I collaborate and consult with other organizational units performing related functions to insure harmonious and efficient working relationships?

12. Do I maintain liaison through prescribed channels with city departments and other governmental agencies concerned with the activities of the unit?

13. Do I maintain contact with and keep abreast of the latest developments and techniques of administration (professional societies, groups, periodicals, etc.) as to their applicability to the activities of the unit?

14. Do I communicate with superiors and subordinates through prescribed organizational channels?

15. Do I notify superiors and subordinates in instances where bypassing is necessary as soon thereafter as practicable?

16. Do I keep my superior informed of significant developments and problems?

SEVEN BASIC FUNCTIONS OF THE SUPERVISOR

I. PLANNING
This means working out goals and means to obtain goals. What needs to be done, who will do it, how, when, and where it is to be done.

SEVEN STEPS IN PLANNING

A. Define job or problem clearly.
B. Consider priority of job.
C. Consider time-limit—starting and completing.
D. Consider minimum distraction to, or interference with, other activities.
E. Consider and provide for contingencies—possible emergencies.
F. Break job down into components.

G. Consider the 5 W's and H:
WHY..........is it necessary to do the job? (Is the purpose clearly defined?)
WHAT........needs to be done to accomplish the defined purpose?
.........is needed to do the job? (Money, materials, etc.)
WHO..........is needed to do the job?
..........will have responsibilities?
WHERE......is the work to be done?
WHEN........is the job to begin and end? (Schedules, etc.)
HOW..........is the job to bed done? (Methods, controls, records, etc.)

II. ORGANIZING

This means dividing up the work, establishing clear lines of responsibility and authority and coordinating efforts to get the job done.

III. STAFFING

The whole personnel function of bringing in and training staff, getting the right man and fitting him to the right job—the job to which he is best suited.

In the normal situation, the supervisor's responsibility regarding staffing normally includes providing accurate job descriptions, that is, duties of the jobs, requirements, education and experience, skills, physical, etc.; assigning the work for maximum use of skills; and proper utilization of the probationary period to weed out unsatisfactory employees.

IV. DIRECTING

Providing the necessary leadership to the group supervised. Important work gets done to the supervisor's satisfaction.

V. COORDINATING

The all-important duty of inter-relating the various parts of the work.
The supervisor is also responsible for controlling the coordinated activities. This means measuring performance according to a time schedule and setting quotas to see that the goals previously set are being reached. Reports from workers should be analyzed, evaluated, and made part of all future plans.

VI. REPORTING

This means proper and effective communication to your superiors, subordinates, and your peers (in definition of the job of the supervisor). Reports should be read and information contained therein should be used, not be filed away and forgotten. Reports should be written in such a way that the desired action recommended by the report is forthcoming.

VII. BUDGETING
This means controlling current costs and forecasting future costs. This forecast is based on past experience, future plans and programs, as well as current costs.

You will note that these seven functions can fall under three topics:

Planning) Make a plan Organizing)	Staffing) Directing) Get things done Controlling)	Reporting) Watch it work Budgeting)

PLANNING TO MEET MANAGEMENT GOALS

I. WHAT IS PLANNING?

A. Thinking a job through before new work is done to determine the best way to do it
B. A method of doing something
C. Ways and means for achieving set goals
D. A means of enabling a supervisor to deliver with a minimum of effort, all details involved in coordinating his work

II. WHO SHOULD MAKE PLANS?

Everybody!
All levels of supervision must plan work. (Top management, heads of divisions or bureaus, first line supervisors, and individual employees.) The higher the level, the more planning required.

III. WHAT ARE THE RESULTS OF POOR PLANNING?

A. Failure to meet deadline
B. Low employee morale
C. Lack of job coordination
D. Overtime is frequently necessary
E. Excessive cost, waste of material and manhours

IV. PRINCIPLES OF PLANNING

A. Getting a clear picture of your objectives. What exactly are you trying to accomplish?
B. Plan the whole job, then the parts, in proper sequence.
C. Delegate the planning of details to those responsible for executing them.
D. Make your plan flexible.
E. Coordinate your plan with the plans of others so that the work may be processed with a minimum of delay.
F. Sell your plan before you execute it.
G. Sell your plan to your superior, subordinate, in order to gain maximum participation and coordination.
H. Your plan should take precedence. Use knowledge and skills that others have brought to a similar job.
I. Your plan should take account of future contingencies; allow for future expansion.
J. Plans should include minor details. Leave nothing to chance that can be anticipated.
K. Your plan should be simple and provide standards and controls. Establish quality and quantity standards and set a standard method of doing the job. The controls will indicate whether the job is proceeding according to plan.
L. Consider possible bottlenecks, breakdowns, or other difficulties that are likely to arise.

V. Q. WHAT ARE THE YARDSTICKS BY WHICH PLANNING SHOULD BE MEASURED?
A. Any plan should:
- —Clearly state a definite course of action to be followed and goal to be achieved, with consideration for emergencies.
- — Be realistic and practical.
- — State what's to be done, when it's to be done, where, how, and by whom.
- — Establish the most efficient sequence of operating steps so that more is accomplished in less time, with the least effort, and with the best quality results.
- — Assure meeting deliveries without delays.
- — Establish the standard by which performance is to be judged.

Q. WHAT KINDS OF PLANS DOES EFFECTIVE SUPERVISION REQUIRE?
A. Plans should cover such factors as:
- — Manpower: right number of properly trained employees on the job
- — Materials: adequate supply of the right materials and supplies
- — Machines: full utilization of machines and equipment, with proper maintenance
- — Methods: most efficient handling of operations
- — Deliveries: making deliveries on time
- — Tools: sufficient well-conditioned tools
- — Layout: most effective use of space
- — Reports: maintaining proper records and reports
- — Supervision: planning work for employees and organizing supervisor's own time

MANAGEMENT PRINCIPLES

I. MANAGEMENT
Q. What do we mean by management?
A. Getting work done through others.

Management could also be defined as planning, directing, and controlling the operations of a bureau or division so that all factors will function properly and all persons cooperate efficiently for a common objective.

II. MANAGEMENT PRINCIPLES

A. There should be a hierarchy—wherein authority and responsibility run upward and downward through several levels—with a broad base at the bottom and a single head at the top.

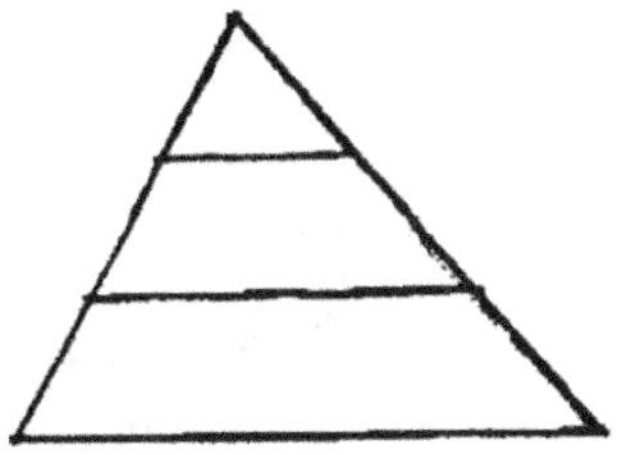

B. Each and every unit or person in the organization should be answerable ultimately to the manager at the apex. In other words, *The buck stops here!*

C. Every necessary function involved in the bureau's objectives is assigned to a unit in that bureau.

D. Responsibilities assigned to a unit are specifically clear-cut and understood.

E. Consistent methods of organizational structure should be applied at each level of the organization.

F. Each member of the bureau from top to bottom knows: to whom he reports and who reports to him.

G. No member of one bureau reports to more than one supervisor. No dual functions.

H. Responsibility for a function is matched by authority necessary to perform that function. Weight of authority.

I. Individuals or units reporting to a supervisor do not exceed the number which can be feasibly and effectively coordinated and directed. Concept of *span of control.*

J. Channels of command (management) are not violated by staff units, although there should be staff services to facilitate and coordinate management functions.

K. Authority and responsibility should be decentralized to units and individuals who are responsible for the actual performance of operations.
Welfare – down to Welfare Centers
Hospitals – down to local hospitals

L. Management should exercise control through attention to policy problems of exceptional performance, rather than through review of routine actions of subordinates.

M. Organizations should never be permitted to grow so elaborate as to hinder work accomplishments.

III. ORGANIZATION STRUCTURE

Types of Organizations
The purest form is a leader and a few followers, such as:

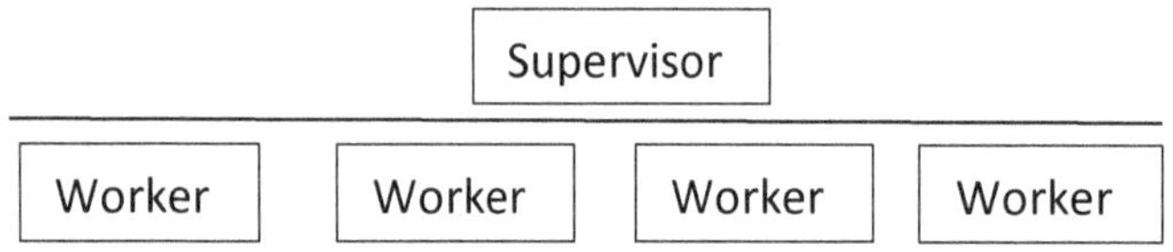

(Refer to organization chart) from supervisor to workers.

The line of authority is direct, The workers know exactly where they stand in relation to their boss, to whom they report for instructions and direction.

Unfortunately, in our present complex society, few organizations are similar to this example of a pure line organization. In this era of specialization, other people are often needed in the simplest of organizations. These specialists are known as staff. The sole purpose for their existence (staff) is to assist, advise, suggest, help or counsel line organizations. Staff has no authority to direct line people—nor do they give them direct instructions.

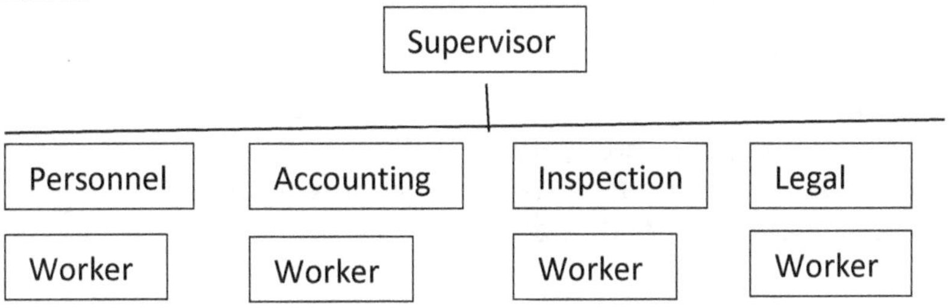

<u>Line Functions</u>

1. Directs
2. Orders
3. Responsibility for carrying out activities from beginning to end
4. Follows chain of command
5. Is identified with what it does
6. Decides when and how to use staff advice
7. Line executes

<u>Staff Functions</u>

1. Advises
2. Persuades and sells
3. Staff studies, reports, recommends but does not carry out
4. May advise across department lines
5. May find its ideas identified with others
6. Has to persuade line to want its advice
7. Staff: Conducts studies and research. Provides advice and instructions in technical matters. Serves as technical specialist to render specific services.

<u>Types and Functions of Organization Charts</u>

An organization chart is a picture of the arrangement and inter-relationship of the subdivisions of an organization.

A. Types of Charts:
   1. Structural: basic relationships only
   2. Functional: includes functions or duties
   3. Personnel: positions, salaries, status, etc.
   4. Process Chart: work performed
   5. Gantt Chart: actual performance against planned
   5. Flow Chart: flow and distribution of work

B. Functions of Charts:
   1. Assist in management planning and control
   2. Indicate duplication of functions
   3. Indicate incorrect stressing of functions
   4. Indicate neglect of important functions
   5. Correct unclear authority
   6. Establish proper span of control

C. Limitations of Charts:
   1. Seldom maintained on current basis
   2. Chart is oversimplified
   3. Human factors cannot adequately be charted

D. Organization Charts should be:
   1. Simple
   2. Symmetrical
   3. Indicate authority
   4. Line and staff relationship differentiated
   5. Chart should be dated and bear signature of approving officer
   6. Chart should be displayed, not hidden

ORGANIZATION

There are four basic principles of organization:

1. Unity of command
2. Span of control
3. Uniformity of assignment
4. Assignment of responsibility and delegation of authority

I. UNITY OF COMMAND

Unity of command means that each person in the organization should receive orders from one, and only one, supervisor. When a person has to take orders from two or more people, (a) the orders may be in conflict and the employee is upset because he does not know which he should obey, or (b) different orders may reach him at the same time and he does not know which he should carry out first.

Equally as bad as having two bosses is the situation where the supervisor is bypassed. Let us suppose you are a supervisor whose boss bypasses you (deals directly with people reporting to you). To the worker, it is the same as having two bosses; but to you, the supervisor, it is equally serious. Bypassing on the part of your boss will undermine your authority, and the people under you will begin looking to your boss for decisions and even for routine orders.

You can prevent bypassing by telling the people you supervise that if anyone tries to give them orders, they should direct that person to you.

II. SPAN OF CONTROL

Span of control on a given level involves:

A. The number of people being supervised
B. The distance
C The time involved in supervising the people. (One supervisor cannot supervise too many workers effectively.)

Span of control means that a supervisor has the right number (not too many and not too few) of subordinates that he can supervise well.

III. UNIFORMITY OF ASSIGNMENT

In assigning work, you as the supervisor should assign to each person jobs that are similar in nature. An employee who is assigned too many different types of jobs will waste time in going from one kind of work to another. It takes time for him to get to top production in one kind of task and, before he does so, he has to start on another.
When you assign work to people, remember that:

A. Job duties should be definite. Make it clear from the beginning what they are to do, how they are to do it, and why they are to do it. Let them know how much they are expected to do and how well they are expected to do it.
B. Check your assignments to be certain that there are no workers with too many unrelated duties, and that no two people have been given overlapping responsibilities. Your aim should be to have every task assigned to a specific person with the work fairly distributed and with each person doing his part.

IV. ASSIGNMENT OF RESPONSIBILITY AND DELEGATION OF AUTHORITY

A supervisor cannot delegate his final responsibility for the work of his department. The experienced supervisor knows that he gets his work done through people. He can't do it all himself. So he must assign the work and the responsibility for the work to his employees. Then they must be given the authority to carry out their responsibilities.

By assigning responsibility and delegating authority to carry out the responsibility, the supervisor builds in his workers initiative, resourcefulness, enthusiasm, and interest in their work. He is treating them as responsible adults. They can find satisfaction in their work, and they will respect the supervisor and be loyal to the supervisor.

PRINCIPLES OF ORGANIZATION

I. DEFINITION

Organization is the method of dividing up the work to provide the best channels for coordinated effort to get the agency's mission accomplished.

II. PURPOSE OF ORGANIZATION

A. To enable each employee within the organization to clearly know his responsibilities and relationships to his fellow employees and to organizational units
B. To avoid conflicts of authority and overlapping of jurisdiction.
C. To ensure teamwork.

III. BASIC CONSIDERATIONS IIN ORGANIZATIONAL PLANNING

A. The basic plans and objectives of the agency should be determined, and the organizational structure should be adapted to carry out effectively such plans and objectives.
B. The organization should be built around the major functions of the agency and not individuals or groups of individuals.

C. The organization should be sufficiently flexible to meet new and changing conditions which may be brought about from within or outside the department.
D. The organizational structure should be as simple as possible and the number of organizational units kept at a minimum.
E. The number of levels of authority should be kept at a minimum. Each additional management level lengthens the chain of authority and responsibility and increases the time for instructions to be distributed to operating levels and for decisions to be obtained from higher authority.
F. The form of organization should permit each executive to exercise maximum initiative within the limits of delegated authority.

IV. BASES FOR ORGANIZATION

A. Purpose (Examples: education, police, sanitation)
B. Process (Examples: accounting, legal, purchasing)
C. Clientele (Examples: welfare, parks, veteran)
D. Geographic (Examples: borough offices, precincts, libraries)

V. ASSIGNMENTS OF FUNCTIONS

A. Every function of the agency should be assigned to a specific organizational unit. Under normal circumstances, no single function should be assigned to more than one organizational unit.
B. There should be no overlapping, duplication, or conflict between organizational elements.
C. Line functions should be separated from staff functions, and proper emphasis should be placed on staff activities.
D. Functions which are closely related or similar should normally be assigned to a single organizational unit.
E. Functions should be properly distributed to promote balance, and to avoid overemphasis of less important functions and underemphasis of more essential functions.

VI. DELEGATION OF AUTHORITY AND RESPONSIBILITY

A. Responsibilities assigned to a specific individual or organizational unit should carry corresponding authority, and all statements of authority or limitations thereof should be as specific as possible.
B. Authority and responsibility for action should be decentralized to organizational units and individuals responsible for actual performance to the greatest extent possible, without relaxing necessary control over policy or the standardization of procedures. Delegation of authority will be consistent with decentralization of responsibility but such delegation will not divest an executive in higher authority of his overall responsibility.
C. The heads of organizational units should concern themselves with important matters and should delegate to the maximum extent details and routines performed in the ordinary course of business.
D. All responsibilities, authorities, and relationships should be stated in simple language to avoid misinterpretation.
E. Each individual or organizational unit charged with a specific responsibility will be held responsible for results.

VII. EMPLOYEE RELATIONSHIPS

A. The employees reporting to one executive should not exceed the number which can be effectively directed and coordinated. The number will depend largely upon the scope and extent of the responsibilities of the subordinates.
B. No person should report to more than one supervisor. Every supervisor should know who reports to him, and every employee should know to whom he reports. Channels of authority and responsibility should not be violated by staff units.
C. Relationships between organizational units within the agency and with outside organizations and associations should be clearly stated and thoroughly understood to avoid misunderstanding.

DELEGATING

I. WHAT IS DELEGATING?
Delegating is assigning a job to an employee, giving him the authority to get that job done, and giving him the responsibility for seeing to it that the job is done.

A. What To Delegate
   1. Routine details
   2. Jobs which may be necessary and take a lot of time, but do not have to be done by the supervisor personally (preparing reports, attending meetings, etc.)
   3. Routine decision-making (making decisions which do not require the supervisor's personal attention)

B. What Not To Delegate
   1. Job details which are *executive functions* (setting goals, organizing employees into a good team, analyzing results so as to plan for the future)
   2. Disciplinary power (handling grievances, preparing service ratings, reprimands, etc.)
   3. Decision-making which involves large numbers of employees or other bureaus and departments
   4. Final and complete responsibility for the job done by the unit being supervised

C. Why Delegate?
   1. To strengthen the organization by developing a greater number of skilled employees
   2. To improve the employee's performance by giving him the chance to learn more about the job, handle some responsibility, and become more interested in getting the job done
   3. To improve a supervisor's performance by relieving him of routine jobs and giving him more time for *executive functions* (planning, organizing, controlling, etc.) which cannot be delegated

II. TO WHOM TO DELEGATE
People with abilities not being used. Selection should be based on ability, not on favoritism.

REPORTS

I. DEFINITION

A report is an orderly presentation of factual information directed to a specific reader for a specific purpose

II. PURPOSE

The general purpose of a report is to bring to the reader useful and factual information about a condition or a problem. Some specific purposes of a report may be:

A. To enable the reader to appraise the efficiency or effectiveness of a person or an operation
B. To provide a basis for establishing standards
C. To reflect the results of expenditures of time, effort, and money
D. To provide a basis for developing or altering programs

III. TYPES

A. Information Report: Contains facts arranged in sequence
B. Summary (Examination) Report: Contains facts plus an analysis or discussion of the significance of the facts. Analysis may give advantages and disadvantages or give qualitative and quantitative comparisons
C. Recommendation Report: Contains facts, analysis, and conclusion logically drawn from the facts and analysis, plus a recommendation based upon the facts, analysis, and conclusions

IV. FACTORS TO CONSIDER BEFORE WRITING REPORT

A. Why write the report?: The purpose of the report should be clearly defined.
B. Who will read the report?: What level of language should be used? Will the reader understand professional or technical language?
C. What should be said?: What does the reader need or want to know about the subject?
D. How should it be said?: Should the subject be presented tactfully? Convincingly? In a stimulating manner?

V. PREPARATORY STEPS

A. Assemble the facts: Find out who, why, what, where, when, and how.
B. Organize the facts: Eliminate unnecessary information
C. Prepare an outline: Check for orderliness, logical sequence
D. Prepare a draft: Check for correctness, clearness, completeness, conciseness, and tone
E. Prepare it in final form: Check for grammar, punctuation, appearance

VI. OUTLINE FOR A RECOMMENDATION REPORT

Is the report:
A. Correct in information, grammar, and tone?
B. Clear?
C. Complete?

D. Concise?
E. Timely?
F. Worth its cost?

Will the report accomplish its purpose?

MANAGEMENT CONTROLS

I. CONTROL

What is control? What is controlled? Who controls?

The essence of control is action which adjusts operations to predetermined standards, and its basis is information in the hands of managers. Control is checking to determine whether plans are being observed and suitable progress toward stated objectives is being made, and action is taken, if necessary, to correct deviations.

We have a ready-made model for this concept of control in the automatic systems which are widely used for process control in the chemical land petroleum industries. A process control system works this way. Suppose, for example, it is desired to maintain a constant rate of flow of oil through a pipe at a predetermined or set-point value. A signal, whose strength represents the rate of flow, can be produced in a measuring device and transmitted to a control mechanism. The control mechanism, when it detects any deviation of the actual from the set-point signal, will reposition the value regulating flow rate.

II. BASIS FOR CONTROL

A process control mechanism thus acts to adjust operations to predetermined standards and does so on the basis of information it receives. In a parallel way, information reaching a manager gives him the opportunity for corrective action and is his basis for control. He cannot exercise control without such information, and he cannot do a complete job of managing without controlling.

III. POLICY

What is policy?

Policy is simply a statement of an organization's intention to act in certain ways when specified types of circumstances arise. It represents a general decision, predetermined and expressed as a principle or rule, establishing a normal pattern of conduct for dealing with given types of business events—usually recurrent. A statement is therefore useful in economizing the time of managers and in assisting them to discharge their responsibilities equitably and consistently.

Policy is not a means of control, but policy does generate the need for control.

Adherence to policies is not guaranteed nor can it be taken on faith. It has to be verified. Without verification, there is no basis for control. Policy and procedures, although closely related and interdependent to a certain extent, are not synonymous. A policy may be adopted, for example, to maintain a materials inventory not to exceed one million dollars.

A procedure for inventory control could interpret that policy and convert it into methods for keeping within that limit, with consideration, too, of possible but foreseeable expedient deviation.

IV. PROCEDURE

What is procedure?

A procedure specifically prescribes:
A. What work is to be performed by the various participants
B. Who are the respective participants
C. When and where the various steps in the different processes are to be performed
D. The sequence of operations that will insure uniform handling of recurring transactions
E. The paper that is involved, its origin, transition, and disposition

Necessary appurtenances to a procedure are:
A. Detailed organizational chart
B. Flow charts
C. Exhibits of forms, all presented in close proximity to the text of the procedure

V. BASIS OF CONTROL – INFORMATION IN THE HANDS OF MANAGERS

If the basis of control is information in the hands of managers, then reporting is elevated to a level of very considerable importance.

Types of reporting may include:
A. Special reports and routine reports
B. Written, oral, and graphic reports
C. Staff meetings
D. Conferences
E. Television screens
F. Non-receipt of information, as where management is by exception
G. Any other means whereby information is transmitted to a manager as a basis for control action

FRAMEWORK OF MANAGEMENT

I. ELEMENTS

A. Policy: It has to be verified, controlled.

B. Organization is part of the giving of an assignment. The organizational chart gives to each individual in his title, a first approximation of the nature of his assignment and orients him as being accountable to a certain individual. Organization is not in a true sense a means of control. Control is checking to ascertain whether the assignment is executed as intended and acting on the basis of that information.

C. Budgets perform three functions:
   1. They present the objectives, plans, and programs of the organization in financial terms.

2. They report the progress of actual performance against these predetermined objectives, plans, and programs.
3. Like organizational charts, delegations of authority, procedures, and job descriptions, they define the assignments which have flowed from the Chief Executive. Budgets are a means of control in the respect that they report progress of actual performance against the program. They provide information which enables managers to take action directed toward bringing actual results into conformity with the program.

D. Internal Check provides in practice for the principle that the same person should not have responsibility for all phases of a transaction. This makes it clearly an aspect of organization rather than of control. Internal Check is static, or built-in.

E. Plans, Programs, Objectives
People must know what they are trying to do. Objectives fulfill this need. Without them, people may work industriously and yet, working aimlessly, accomplish little. Plans and Programs complement Objectives, since they propose how and according to what time schedule the objectives are to be reached.

F. Delegations of Authority
Among the ways we have for supplementing the titles and lines of authority of an organizational chart are delegations of authority. Delegations of authority clarify the extent of authority of individuals and in that way serve to define assignments. That they are not means of control is apparent from the very fact that wherever there has been a delegation of authority, the need for control increases. This could hardly be expected to happen if delegations of authority were themselves means of control.

II. MANAGER'S RESPONSIBILITY

Control becomes necessary whenever a manager delegates authority to a subordinate because he cannot delegate and then simply sit back and forget4 about it. A manager's accountability to his own superior has not diminished one whit as a result of delegating part of his authority to a subordinate. The manager must exercise control over actions taken under the authority so delegated. That means checking serves as a basis for possible corrective action.

Objectives, plans, programs, organizational charts, and other elements of the managerial system are not fruitfully regarded as either controls or means of control. They are pre-established standards or models of performance to which operations are adjusted by the exercise of management control. These standards or models of performance are dynamic in character for they are constantly altered, modified, or revised. Policies, organizational set-up, procedures, delegations, etc. are constantly altered but, like objectives and plans, they remain in force until they are either abandoned or revised. All of the elements (or standards or models of performance), objectives, plans, and programs, policies, organization, etc. can be regarded as a *framework of management*.

III. CONTROL TECHNIQUES

Examples of control techniques:

A. Compare against established standards
B. Compare with a similar operation
C. Compare with past operations
D. Compare with predictions of accomplishment

IV. WHERE FORECASTS FIT

Control is after-the-fact while forecasts are before. Forecasts and projections are important for setting objectives and formulating plans.

Information for aiming and planning does not have to be before-the-fact. It may be an after-the-fact analysis proving that a certain policy has been impolitic in its effect on the relation of the company or department with customer, employee, taxpayer, or stockholder; or that a certain plan is no longer practical, or that a certain procedure is unworkable.

The prescription here certainly would not be in control (in these cases, control would simply bring operations into conformity with obsolete standards) but the establishment of new standards, a new policy, a new plan, and a new procedure to be controlled too.

Information is, of course, the basis for all communication in addition to furnishing evidence to management of the need for reconstructing the framework of management.

PROBLEM SOLVING

The accepted concept in modern management for problem solving is the utilization of the following steps:

A. Identify the problem
B. Gather data
C. List possible solutions
D. Test possible solutions
E. Select the best solution
F. Put the solution into actual practice

Occasions might arise where you would have to apply the second step of gathering data before completing the first step.

You might also find that it will be necessary to work on several steps at the same time.

I. IDENTIFY THE PROBLEM

Your first step is to define as precisely as possible the problem to be solved. While this may sound easy, it is often the most difficult part of the process.

It has been said of problem solving that you are halfway to the solution when you can write out a clear statement of the problem itself.

Our job now is to get below the surface manifestations of the trouble and pinpoint the problem. This is usually accomplished by a logical analysis, by going from the general to the particular; from the obvious to the not-so-obvious cause.

Let us say that production is behind schedule. WHY? Absenteeism is high. Now, is absenteeism the basic problem to be tackled, or is it merely a symptom of low morale among the workforce? Under these circumstances, you may decide that production is not the problem; the problem is *employee morale*.

In trying to define the problem, remember there is seldom one simple reason why production is lagging, or reports are late, etc.

Analysis usually leads to the discovery that an apparent problem is really made up of several subproblems which must be attacked separately.

Another way is to limit the problem, and thereby ease the task of finding a solution, and concentrate on the elements which are within the scope of your control.

When you have gone this far, write out a tentative statement of the problem to be solved.

II. GATHER DATA

In the second step, you must set out to collect all the information that might have a bearing on the problem. Do not settle for an assumption when reasonable fact and figures are available.

If you merely go through the motions of problem-solving, you will probably shortcut the information-gathering step. Therefore, do not stack the evidence by confining your research to your own preconceived ideas.

As you collect facts, organize them in some form that helps you make sense of them and spot possible relationships between them. For example, plotting cost per unit figures on a graph can be more meaningful than a long column of figures.

Evaluate each item as you go along. Is the source material absolutely, reliable, probably reliable, or not to be trusted.

One of the best methods for gathering data is to go out and look the situation over carefully. Talk to the people on the job who are most affected by this problem.

Always keep in mind that a primary source is usually better than a secondary source of information.

III. LIST POSSIBLE SOLUTIONS

This is the creative thinking step of problem solving. This is a good time to bring into play whatever techniques of group dynamics the agency or bureau might have developed for a joint attack on problems.

Now the important thing for you to do is: Keep an open mind. Let your imagination roam freely over the facts you have collected. Jot down every possible solution that occurs to you. Resist the temptation to evaluate various proposals as you go along. List seemingly absurd ideas along with more plausible ones. The more possibilities you list during this step, the less risk you will run of settling for merely a workable, rather than the best, solution.

Keep studying the data as long as there seems to be any chance of deriving additional ideas, solutions, explanations, or patterns from it.

IV. TEST POSSIBLE SOLUTIONS

Now you begin to evaluate the possible solutions. Take pains to be objective. Up to this point, you have suspended judgment but you might be tempted to select a solution you secretly favored all along and proclaim it as the best of the lot.

The secret of objectivity in this phase is to test the possible solutions separately, measuring each against a common yardstick. To make this yardstick try to enumerate as many specific criteria as you can think of. Criteria are best phrased as questions which you ask of each possible solution. They can be drawn from these general categories:

Suitability – Will this solution do the job?
Will it solve the problem completely or partially?
Is it a permanent or a stopgap solution?

Feasibility - Will this plan work in actual practice?
Can we afford this approach?
How much will it cost?

Acceptability - Will the boss go along with the changes required in the plan?
Are we trying to drive a tack with a sledge hammer?

V. SELECT THE BEST SOLUTION

This is the area of executive decision.

Occasionally, one clearly superior solution will stand out at the conclusion of the testing process. But often it is not that simple. You may find that no one solution has come through all the tests with flying colors.

You may also find that a proposal, which flunked miserably on one of the essential tests, racked up a very high score on others.

The best solution frequently will turn out to be a combination.

Try to arrange a marriage that will bring together the strong points of one possible solution with the particular virtues of another. The more skill and imagination that you apply, the greater is the likelihood that you will come out with a solution that is not merely adequate and workable, but is the best possible under the circumstances.

VI. PUT THE SOLUTION INTO ACTUAL PRACTICE

As every executive knows, a plan which works perfectly on paper may develop all sorts of bugs when put into actual practice.

Problem-solving does not stop with selecting the solution which looks best in theory. The next step is to put the chosen solution into action and watch the results. The results may point towards modifications.

If the problem disappears when you put your solution into effect, you know you have the right solution.

If it does not disappear, even after you have adjusted your plan to cover unforeseen difficulties that turned up in practice, work your way back through the problem-solving solutions.

Would one of them have worked better?
Did you overlook some vital piece of data which would have given you a different slant on the whole situation? Did you apply all necessary criteria in testing solutions? If no light dawns after this much rechecking, it is a pretty good bet that you defined the problem incorrectly in the first place.

You came up with the wrong solution because you tackled the wrong problem.

Thus, step six may become step one of a new problem-solving cycle.

COMMUNICATION

I. WHAT IS COMMUNICATION?
We communicate through writing, speaking, action, or inaction. In speaking to people face-to-face, there is opportunity to judge reactions and to adjust the message. This makes the supervisory chain one of the most, and in many instances the most, important channels of communication.

In an organization, communication means keeping employees informed about the organization's objectives, policies, problems, and progress. Communication is the free interchange of information, ideas, and desirable attitudes between and among employees and between employees and management.

II. WHY IS COMMUNICATION NEEDED?

A. People have certain social needs
B. Good communication is essential in meeting those social needs
C. While people have similar basic needs, at the same time they differ from each other
D. Communication must be adapted to these individual differences

An employee cannot do his best work unless he knows why he is doing it. If he has the feeling that he is being kept in the dark about what is going on, his enthusiasm and productivity suffer.

Effective communication is needed in an organization so that employees will understand what the organization is trying to accomplish; and how the work of one unit contributes to or affects the work of other units in the organization and other organizations.

III. HOW IS COMMUNICATION ACHIEVED?

Communication flows downward, upward, sideways.

A. Communication may come from top management down to employees. This is downward communication.

   Some means of downward communication are:
   1. Training (orientation, job instruction, supervision, public relations, etc.)
   2. Conferences
   3. Staff meetings
   4. Policy statements
   5. Bulletins
   6. Newsletters
   7. Memoranda
   8. Circulation of important letters

   In downward communication, it is important that employees be informed in advance of changes that will affect them.

B. Communications should also be developed so that the ideas, suggestions, and knowledge of employees will flow upward to top management.

   Some means of upward communication are:
   1. Personal discussion conferences
   2. Committees
   3. Memoranda
   4. Employees suggestion program
   5. Questionnaires to be filled in giving comments and suggestions about proposed actions that will affect field operations.

   Upward communication requires that management be willing to listen, to accept, and to make changes when good ideas are present. Upward communication succeeds when there is no fear of punishment for speaking out or lack of interest at the top. Employees will share their knowledge and ideas with management when interest is shown and recognition is given.

C. The advantages of downward communication:
   1. It enables the passing down of orders, policies, and plans necessary to the continued operation of the station.
   2. By making information available, it diminishes the fears and suspicions which result from misinformation and misunderstanding.
   3. It fosters the pride people want to have in their work when they are told of good work.
   4. It improves the morale and stature of the individual to be *in the know.*

5. It helps employees to understand, accept, and cooperate with changes when they know about them in advance.

D. The advantages of upward communication:
   1. It enables the passing upward of information, attitudes, and feelings.
   2. It makes it easier to find out how ready people are to receive downward communication.
   3. It reveals the degree to which the downward communication is understood and accepted.
   4. It helps to satisfy the basic social needs.
   5. It stimulates employees to participate in the operation of their organization.
   6. It encourage employees to contribute ideas for improving the efficiency and economy of operations.
   7. It helps to solve problem situations before they reach the explosion point.

IV. WHY DOES COMMUNICATION FAIL?

A. The technical difficulties of conveying information clearly
B. The emotional content of communication which prevents complete transmission
C. The fact that there is a difference between what management needs to say, what it wants to day, and what it does say
D. The fact that there is a difference between what employees would like to say, what they think is profitable or safe to say, and what they do say

V. HOW TO IMPROVE COMMUNICATION

As a supervisor, you are a key figure in communication. To improve as a communicator, you should:

A. Know: Knowing your subordinates will help you to recognize and work with individual differences.
B. Like: If you like those who work for you and those for whom you work, this will foster the kind of friendly, warm, work atmosphere that will facilitate communication.
C. Trust: Showing a sincere desire to communicate will help to develop the mutual trust and confidence which are essential to the free flow of communication.
D. Tell: Tell your subordinates and superiors *what's doing*. Tell your subordinates *why* as well as *how*.
E. Listen: By listening, you help others to talk and you create good listeners. Don't forget that listening implies action.
F. Stimulate: Communication has to be stimulated and encouraged. Be receptive to ideas and suggestions and motivate your people so that each member of the team identifies himself with the job at hand.
G. Consult: The most effective way of consulting is to let your people participate, insofar as possible, in developing determinations which affect them or their work.

VI. HOW TO DETERMINE WHETHER YOU ARE GETTING ACROSS

A. Check to see that communication is received and understood
B. Judge this understanding by actions rather than words
C. Adapt or vary communication, when necessary
D. Remember that good communication cannot cure all problems

VII. THE KEY ATTITUDE

Try to see things from the other person's point of view. By doing this, you help to develop the permissive atmosphere and the shared confidence and understanding which are essential to effective two-way communication.

Communication is a two-way process:
A. The basic purpose of any communication is to get action.
B. The only way to get action is through acceptance.
C. In order to get acceptance, communication must be humanly satisfying as well as technically efficient.

HOW ORDERS AND INSTRUCTIONS SHOULD BE GIVEN

I. CHARACTERISTICS OF GOOD ORDERS AND INSTRUCTIONS

A. Clear
Orders should be definite as to
—What is to be done
—Who is to do it
—When it is to be done
—Where it is to be done
—How it is to be done

B. Concise
Avoid wordiness. Orders should be brief and to the point.

C. Timely
Instructions and orders should be sent out at the proper time and not too long in advance of expected performance.

D. Possibility of Performance
Orders should be feasible:
1. Investigate before giving orders
2. Consult those who are to carry out instructions before formulating and issuing them

E. Properly Directed
Give the orders to the people concerned. Do not send orders to people who are not concerned. People who continually receive instructions that are not applicable to them get in the habit of neglecting instructions generally.

F. Reviewed Before Issuance
Orders should be reviewed before issuance:
1. Test them by putting yourself in the position of the recipient
2. If they involve new procedures, have the persons who are to do the work review them for suggestions.

G. Reviewed After Issuance
Persons who receive orders should be allowed to raise questions and to point out unforeseen consequences of orders.

H. Coordinated
Orders should be coordinated so that work runs smoothly.

I. Courteous
Make a request rather than a demand. There is no need to continually call attention to the fact that you are the boss.

J. Recognizable as an Order
Be sure that the order is recognizable as such.

K. Complete
Be sure recipient has knowledge and experience sufficient to carry out order. Give illustrations and examples.

A DEPARTMENTAL PERSONNEL OFFICE IS RESPONSIBLE FOR THE FOLLOWING FUNCTIONS

1. Policy
2. Personnel Programs
3. Recruitment and Placement
4. Position Classification
5. Salary and Wage Administration
6. Employee performance Standards and Evaluation
7. Employee Relations
8. Disciplinary Actions and Separations
9. Health and Safety
10. Staff Training and Development
11. Personnel Records, Procedures, and Reports
12. Employee Services
13. Personnel Research

SUPERVISION

I. LEADERSHIP

All leadership is based essentially on authority. This comes from two sources: It is received from higher management or it is earned by the supervisor through his methods of supervision. Although effective leadership has always depended upon the leader's using his authority in such a way as to appeal successfully to the motives of the people supervised, the conditions for making this appeal are continually changing. The key to today's problem of leadership is flexibility and resourcefulness on the part of the leader in meeting changes in conditions as they occur.

Three basic approaches to leadership are generally recognized:

A. The Authoritarian Approach
   1. The methods and techniques used in this approach emphasize the *I* in leadership and depend primarily on the formal authority of the leader. This authority is sometimes exercised in a hardboiled manner and sometimes in a benevolent

manner, but in either case the dominating role of the leader is reflected in the thinking, planning, and decisions of the group.

2. Group results are to a large degree dependent on close supervision by the leader. Usually, the individuals in the group will not show a high degree of initiative or acceptance of responsibility and their capacity to grow and develop probably will not be fully utilized. The group may react with resentment or submission, depending upon the manner and skill of the leader in using his authority.
3. This approach develops as a natural outgrowth of the authority that goes with the leader's job and his feeling of sole responsibility for getting the job done. It is relatively easy to use and does not require must resourcefulness.
4. The use of this approach is effective in times of emergencies, in meeting close deadline as a final resort, in settling some issues, in disciplinary matters, and with dependent individuals and groups.

B. The Laissez-Faire or Let 'em Alone Approach

1. This approach generally is characterized by an avoidance of leadership responsibility by the leader. The activities of the group depend largely on the choice of its members rather than the leader.
2. Group results probably will be poor. Generally, there will be disagreements over petty things, bickering, and confusion. Except for a few aggressive people, individuals will not show much initiative and growth and development will be retarded. There may be a tendency for informal leaders to take over leadership of the group.
3. This approach frequently results from the leader's dislike of responsibility, from his lack of confidence, from failure of other methods to work, from disappointment or criticism. It is usually the easiest of the three to use and requires both understanding and resourcefulness on the part of the leader.
4. This approach is occasionally useful and effective, particularly in forcing dependent individuals or groups to rely on themselves, to give someone a chance to save face by clearing his own difficulties, or when action should be delayed temporarily for good cause.

C. The Democratic Approach

1. The methods and techniques used in this approach emphasize the *we* in leadership and build up the responsibility of the group to attain its objectives. Reliance is placed largely on the earned authority of the leader.
2. Group results are likely to be good because most of the job motives of the people will be satisfied. Cooperation and teamwork, initiative, acceptance of responsibility, and the individual's capacity for growth probably will show a high degree of development.
3. This approach grows out of a desire or necessity of the leader to find ways to appeal effectively to the motivation of his group. It is the best approach to build up inside the person a strong desire to cooperate and apply himself to the job. It is the most difficult to develop, and requires both understanding and resourcefulness on the part of the leader.
4. The value of this approach increases over a long period where sustained efficiency and development of people are important. It may not be fully effective in all situations, however, particularly when there is not sufficient time to use it properly or where quick decisions must be made.

All three approaches are used by most leaders and have a place in supervising people. The extent of their use varies with individual leaders, with some using one approach predominantly. The leader who uses these three approaches, and varies their use with time and circumstance, is probably the most effective. Leadership which is used predominantly with a democratic approach requires more resourcefulness on the part of the leader but offers the greatest possibilities in terms of teamwork and cooperation.

The one best way of developing democratic leadership is to provide a real sense of participation on the part of the group, since this satisfies most of the chief job motives. Although there are many ways of providing participation, consulting as frequently as possible with individuals and groups on things that affect them seems to offer the most in building cooperation and responsibility. Consultation takes different forms, but it is most constructive when people feel they are actually helping in finding the answers to the problems on the job.

There are some requirements of leaders in respect to human relations which should be considered in their selection and development. Generally, the leader should be interested in working with other people, emotionally stable, self-confident, and sensitive to the reactions of others. In addition, his viewpoint should be one of getting the job done through people who work cooperatively in response to his leadership. He should have a knowledge of individual and group behavior, but, most important of all, he should work to combine all of these requirements into a definite, practical skill in leadership.

II. NINE POINTS OF CONTRAST BETWEEN *BOSS* AND *LEADER*

A. The boss drives his men; the leader coaches them.
B. The boss depends on authority; the leader on good will.
C. The boss inspires fear; the leader inspires enthusiasm.
D. The boss says I; the leader says *We*.
E. The boss says *Get here on time*; the leader gets there ahead of time.
F. The boss fixes the blame for the breakdown; the leader fixes the breakdown.
G. The boss knows how it is done; the leader shows how.
H. The boss makes work a drudgery; the leader makes work a game.
I. The boss says *Go*; the leader says *Let's go*.

EMPLOYEE MORALE

Employee morale is the way employees feel about each other, the organization or unit in which they work, and the work they perform.

I. SOME WAYS TO DEVELOP AND MAINTAIN GOOD EMPLYEE MORALE

A. Give adequate credit and praise when due.
B. Recognize importance of all jobs and equalize load with proper assignments, always giving consideration to personality differences and abilities.
C. Welcome suggestions and do not have an *all-wise* attitude. Request employees' assistance in solving problems and use assistants when conducting group meetings on certain subjects.
D. Properly assign responsibilities and give adequate authority for fulfillment of such assignments.

E. Keep employees informed about matters that affect them.
F. Criticize and reprimand employees privately.
G. Be accessible and willing to listen.
H. Be fair.
I. Be alert to detect training possibilities so that you will not miss an opportunity to help each employee do a better job, and if possible with less effort on his part.
J. Set a good example.
K. Apply the golden rule.

II. SOME INDICATIONS OF GOOD MORALE

A. Good quality of work
B. Good quantity
C. Good attitude of employees
D. Good discipline
E. Teamwork
F. Good attendance
G. Employee participation

MOTIVATION

DRIVES

A drive, stated simply, is a desire or force which causes a person to do or say certain things. These are some of the most usual drives and some of their identifying characteristics recognizable in people motivated by such drives:

A. Security (desire to provide for the future)
Always on time for work
Works for the same employer for many years
Never takes unnecessary chances
Seldom resists doing what he is told

B. Recognition (desire to be rewarded for accomplishment)
Likes to be asked for his opinion
Becomes very disturbed when he makes a mistake
Does things to attract attention
Likes to see his name in print

C. Position (desire to hold certain status in relation to others)
Boasts about important people he knows
Wants to be known as a key man
Likes titles
Demands respect
Belongs to clubs, for prestige

D. Accomplishment (desire to get things done)
Complains when things are held up
Likes to do things that have tangible results
Never lies down on the job
Is proud of turning out good work

E. Companionship (desire to associate with other people)
Likes to work with others
Tells stories and jokes
Indulges in horseplay
Finds excuses to talk to others on the job

F. Possession (desire to collect and hoard objects)
Likes to collect things
Puts his name on things belonging to him
Insists on the same location

Supervisors may find that identifying the drives of employees is a helpful step toward motivating them to self-improvement and better job performance. For example: An employee's job performance is below average. His supervisor, having previously determined that the employee is motivated by a drive for security, suggests that taking training courses will help the employee to improve, advance, and earn more money. Since earning more money can be a step toward greater security, the employee's drive for security would motivate him to take the training suggested by the supervisor. In essence, this is the process of charting an employee's future course by using his motivating drives to positive advantage.

EMPLOYEE PARTICIPATION

I. WHAT IS PARTICIPATION

Employee participation is the employee's giving freely of his time, skill, and knowledge to an extent which cannot be obtained by demand.

II. WHY IS IT IMPORTANT?

The supervisor's responsibility is to get the job done through people. A good supervisor gets the job done through people who work willingly and well. The participation of employees is important because:

A. Employees develop a greater sense of responsibility when they share in working out operating plans and goals.
B. Participation provides greater opportunity and stimulation for employees to learn, and to develop their ability.
C. Participation sometimes provides better solutions to problems because such solutions may combine the experience and knowledge of interested employees who want the solutions to work.
D. An employee or group may offer a solution which the supervisor might hesitate to make for fear of demanding too much.

E. Since the group wants to make the solution work, they exert pressure in a constructive way on each other.
F. Participation usually results in reducing the need for close supervision.

II. HOW MAY SUPERVISORS OBTAIN IT?

Participation is encouraged when employees feel that they share some responsibility for the work and that their ideas are sincerely wanted and valued. Some ways of obtaining employee participation are:

A. Conduct orientation programs for new employees to inform them about the organization and their rights and responsibilities as employees.
B. Explain the aims and objectives of the agency. On a continuing basis, be sure that the employees know what these aims and objectives are.
C. Share job successes and responsibilities and give credit for success.
D. Consult with employees, both as individuals and in groups, about things that affect them.
E. Encourage suggestions for job improvements. Help employees to develop good suggestions. The suggestions can bring them recognition. The city's suggestion program offers additional encouragement through cash awards.

The supervisor who encourages employee participation is not surrendering his authority. He must still make decisions and initiate action, and he must continue to be ultimately responsible for the work of those he supervises. But, through employee participation, he is helping his group to develop greater ability and a sense of responsibility while getting the job done faster and better.

STEPS IN HANDLING A GRIEVANCE

1. Get the Facts
   a. Listen sympathetically
   b. Let him talk himself out
   c. Get his story straight
   d. Get his point of view
   e. Don't argue with him
   f. Give him plenty of time
   g. Conduct the interview privately
   h. Don't try to shift the blame or pass the buck

2. Consider the Facts
   a. Consider the employee's viewpoint
   b. How will the decision affect similar cases
   c. Consider each decision as a possible precedent
   d. Avoid snap judgments—don't jump to conclusions

3. Make or Get a Decision
   a. Frame an effective counter-proposal
   b. Make sure it is fair to all
   c. Have confidence in your judgment
   d. Be sure you can substantiate your decision

4. Notify the Employee of Your Decision
Be sure he is told; try to convince him that the decision is fair and just.

5. Take Action When Needed and If Within Your Authority
Otherwise, tell employee that the matter will be called to the attention of the proper person or that nothing can be done, and why it cannot.

6. Follow through to see that the desired result is achieved.

7. Record key facts concerning the complaint and the action taken.

8. Leave the way open to him to appeal your decision to a higher authority.

9. Report all grievances to your superior, whether they are appealed or not.

DISCIPLINE

Discipline is training that develops self-control, orderly conduct, and efficiency.

To discipline does not necessarily mean to punish.

To discipline does mean to train, to regulate, and to govern conduct.

I. THE DISCIPLINARY INTERVIEW

Most employees sincerely want to do what is expected of them. In other words, they are self-disciplined. Some employees, however, fail to observe established rules and standards, and disciplinary action by the supervisor is required.

The primary purpose of disciplinary action is to improve conduct without creating dissatisfaction, bitterness, or resentment in the process.

Constructive disciplinary action is more concerned with causes and explanations of breaches of conduct than with punishment. The disciplinary interview is held to get at the causes of apparent misbehavior and to motivate better performance in the future.

It is important that the interview be kept on an impersonal a basis as possible. If the supervisor lets the interview descend to the plane of an argument, it loses its effectiveness.

II. PLANNING THE INTERVIEW

Get all pertinent facts concerning the situation so that you can talk in specific terms to the employee.

Review the employee's record, appraisal ratings, etc.

Consider what you know about the temperament of the employee. Consider your attitude toward the employee. Remember that the primary requisite of disciplinary action is fairness.

Don't enter upon the interview when angry.

Schedule the interview for a place which is private and out of hearing of others.

III. CONDUCTING THE INTERVIEW

A. Make an effort to establish accord.
B. Question the employee about the apparent breach of discipline. Be sure that the question is not so worded as to be itself an accusation.
C. Give the employee a chance to tell his side of the story. Give him ample opportunity to talk.
D. Use understanding—listening except where it is necessary to ask a question or to point out some details of which the employee may not be aware. If the employee misrepresents facts, make a plain, accurate statement of the facts, but don't argue and don't engage in personal controversy.
E. Listen and try to understand the reasons for the employee's (mis)conduct. First of all, don't assume that there has been a breach of discipline. Evaluate the employee's reasons for his conduct in the light of his opinions and feelings concerning the consistency and reasonableness of the standards which he was expected to follow. Has the supervisor done his part in explaining the reasons for the rule? Was the employee's behavior unintentional or deliberate? Does he think he had real reasons for his actions? What new facts is he telling? Do the facts justify his actions? What causes, other than those mentioned, could have stimulated the behavior?
F. After listening to the employee's version of the situation, and if censure of his actions is warranted, the supervisor should proceed with whatever criticism is justified. Emphasis should be placed on future improvement rather than exclusively on the employee's failure to measure up to expected standards of job conduct.
G. Fit the criticism to the individual. With one employee, a word of correction may be all that is required.
H. Attempt to distinguish between unintentional error and deliberate misbehavior. An error due to ignorance requires training and not censure.
I. Administer criticism in a controlled, even tone of voice, never in anger. Make it clear that you are acting as an agent of the department. In general, criticism should refer to the job or the employee's actions and not to the person. Criticism of the employee's work is not an attack on the individual.
J. Be sure the interview does not destroy the employee's self-confidence. Mention his good qualities and assure him that you feel confident that he can improve his performance.
K. Wherever possible, before the employee leaves the interview, satisfy him that the incident is closed, that nothing more will be said on the subject unless the offense is repeated.

www.ingramcontent.com/pod-product-compliance
Lightning Source LLC
Chambersburg PA
CBHW081819300426
44116CB00014B/2423
* 9 7 8 1 7 9 9 3 1 7 5 4 8 *